D0625759

URBANISM
as
DELINQUENCY

Compromising The Agenda
For Social Change

William J. Mackey, Ph.D.
Professor, Department of Sociology and Archaeology, University of Wisconsin—La Crosse, La Crosse, Wisconsin

Janet Fredericks, Ph.D.
Professor, College of Education, Northeastern Illinois University, Chicago, Illinois

Marcel A. Fredericks, Ph.D.
Professor and Director, Office of Research in Medical Sociology, Department of Sociology and Anthropology, Loyola University of Chicago, Chicago, Illinois

UNIVERSITY
PRESS OF
AMERICA

Lanham • New York • London

Copyright © 1993 by
University Press of America®, Inc.
4720 Boston Way
Lanham, Maryland 20706

3 Henrietta Street
London WC2E 8LU England

All rights reserved
Printed in the United States of America
British Cataloging in Publication Information Available

Library of Congress Cataloging-in-Publication Data

Mackey, William J., professor.
Urbanism as delinquency : compromising the agenda for social
change / William J. Mackey, Janet Fredericks, Marcel A. Fredericks.
p.   cm.
Includes bibliographical references and indexes.
1. Juvenile delinquency.   2. Juvenile delinquency—United
States—Case studies.   I. Fredericks, Janet.
II. Fredericks, Marcel A.   III. Title.
HV9069.M32   1993   364.3'6'0973—dc20   93–7427 CIP

ISBN 0–8191–9102–7 (cloth : alk. paper)
ISBN 0–8191–9103–5 (pbk. : alk. paper)

 The paper used in this publication meets the minimum requirements of
American National Standard for Information Sciences—Permanence
of Paper for Printed Library Materials, ANSI Z39.48–1984.

Backward, turn backward, O Time
      in your flight,
Make me a child again,
      just for to-night!

Elizabeth Akers Allen
(1832-1911)

dedicated to our families

Contents

FOREWORD

URBANISM AS DELINQUENCY

Urbanism as Delinquency is an invaluable eye-opener for the large number of persons engaged in one way or another with delinquents. It gives the reader a spate of penetrating insights from unusual angles so that it is invaluable not only for correctional workers but also for teachers and counselors, for parents, lawyers, ministers and community policy makers of all kinds at all levels.

It is a really refreshing respite from "quanto-phrenia." It is fascinating reading as well because it reads like a play and engages the reader in a dialogue. The chapter headings are flushed out dramatically; thus it captivates and creates interest climactically. Meanwhile a thesis is developed trenchantly; i.e., that delinquency is one of a set of dispersed norms, social relationships and an urban way of life that do not fit well. In the process of doing this more than one Gordian knot is cut; e.g., between the "compassionate" and "just deserts" schools of thought. In dealing with juvenile delinquency as a fractured way of life, of coping with contemporary city living, it in no way takes away from the serious nature of offenses against person and property.

The interpretations are scintillating and are inter-laden with concrete illustrations that clearly illuminate problems and dilemmas. The recommendations are provocative, stimulating and profitable in the context of an excellent run-down and evaluation of competing theories.

As an educator over the last fifty years; I recommend it as a treasure trove for all educators in and outside the fields of correctional work.

John W. Wozniak, Ph.D., L.L.D.
Professor Dean Emeritus
School of Education
Loyola University of Chicago
Chicago, Illinois

1
The Setting

In 1938 Louis Wirth authored a short article published in the *American Journal of Sociology*. While emphasizing urbanism as a " way of life" -- the title itself -- Wirth drew attention to his conclusions that closeness of living arrangements (density) and variegated patterns of getting things done (heterogeneity) had combined to make a different sort of person in recent American history. The population size of American cities had undergone an almost exponential growth in the late nineteenth and early twentieth centuries, due in large part to European immigration. The technological changes accompanying the latter period of the Industrial Revolution, particularly as they related to mass production and assembly, had assured demands for a labor force that was to become increasingly task specific. Work experience would increasingly become evaluated *qualitatively*.

A way of explaining urbanism developed by pointing to what urbanism was *not* -- mostly rurality. Since the movement from an agrarian to an industrial base was recent in the memory of most Americans, the meaning of urbanism was more or less comprehended; it was the antithesis of farm life! It became at once a psychological frame of reference (alienated, lonely) with a sociological standpoint (anomic persons; marginal men). Following Wirth's lead were a number of scholars who emphasized life styles that meshed with city living. Most concentrated on the social problems that appeared inherent and endemic to urban life and culture. Trained as those early sociologists were in the prevailing social science theory and method of the time, social problems were viewed as most dysfunctional to the social fabric; to be rooted out as expeditiously as possible. Few drew attention to the positive and creative part of city life.[1]

Wirth's article was probably most important for its diversion from the tradition of the then current sociology. Although he was of the University of Chicago, his thesis was in itself an oblique critique of what was known as the Chicago School of Sociology. That emphasis dominated the American discipline of Sociology. The Chicago School heavily emphasized the variable of *place* as the key factor to be reckoned with in explanations of events of man. Scholars of the day were quite obviously following the lead of biology, where Ernst Haeckel (1868) had coined the term *Ecology*, which in essence was the observation that organisms are affected by, and in turn affect, their surroundings; observed actions are seen as coping mechanisms. For a long time students referred to a kind of "human ecology" which was a parallel to biological concerns and predictions.

Although Wirth began to challenge the Chicago School's heavy reliance on the *place* factor in explaining human events, we believe it is highly unlikely that the scholars of the sociological tradition were as entirely enamored with this key explanatory factor as they have been accused of being. However, *they were interpreted* that way. Public policy implementors in particular reacted to the Chicago School "as if" there were clear mandates for action. The notion was taken that *problems* could be solved by paying attention to, arranging -- and rearranging -- the place.[2]

Social "tinkering" took on a new life with the message that people could be changed by rearranging their environment -- whether it was whole neighborhoods, houses, or even institutional living. Even the popular literature and Hollywood versions of real life gave homage to this basic idea of the Chicago School. One of Humphrey Bogart's least remembered acting portrayals was in the film "Knock on Any Door", the main theme of which was that crime, delinquency and all sorts of social problems are attributable to the place of residence and neighborhood of orientation. The idea that the slum was the breeding ground of social problems became very surely accepted.

Historians of contemporary criminology would note that attempts to modify behavior by way of physical rearrangements of the place might call attention to similarities of the last century. Certainly the Quaker implementation of "penitential" surroundings for convicts was one of them. The first known Penitentiaries in Pennsylvania offered high hopes of reform based on physical manipulation of the everyday place of social living.

But the scope of social/physical planning was to reach new heights. Particularly following the close of WWII, we witnessed public housing policy that was to see its fulfillment in the numerous projects that were built mostly for the urban poor, but concomitantly for those at risk to the social problems of crime, delinquency, broken families, and the like.

Correctional institutions -- mostly on the U.S. West Coast -- were erected that had as a central purpose changing attitudes and behavior through close exposure to the "good life". This "good life" was sometimes criticized as being overly representative of middle class values; values that portrayed a particular type of goal and dream. An unanticipated consequence of building "nice" correctional facilities was that the various affected authorities and locations were much more willing to make demands on their use and, eventually, over-use. After all, from a tour of facilities one could only conclude that these were pleasant places. It wasn't long before we saw increases in the rates of confinement that kept going skyward. Such was the decade (plus) of that period of the late forties, thru the nineteen-fifties and into the early sixties.

Ecological social planning and problem solving were on an even more grandiose scale. Not only was architecture to be the main tool of rearranging the place; new technologies went hand in hand with building. In urban high-rise public housing, violent assault crime was supposedly to be diminished with such devices as the "skip-stop" elevator: no bank of a building's elevators would have more than one exiting at any given floor at a time. The ubiquity of graffiti and urine would be diminished through the installation of modern ceramics, stainless steel, and stucco type of wall coverings. "One way" mirror windows would cut down crime-delinquency because "someone was always watching." And all of this produced the added bonus of being "cheaper" since it eliminated or at least cut down on human interaction; additional employees would not be needed to be the watch keepers.

None of this really worked, and in what has become a kind of testimonial to its failure, the St. Louis Urban housing development (Pruitt-Igoe) had to be dismantled (demolished -- dynamited) in 1973 after a relatively brief kind of experiment in the social engineering of place -- architecture and technology. (Palen 1975:259-61) Louis Wirth would probably have warned: ". . . I told you so! Pay attention to urbanism as a way of living."

Urbanologist Jane Jacobs has placed much of her advice on urban planning and renewal close to the heart of safety from crime and delinquency. (Palen 1975:255-56) She too followed the Chicago School's often implied connection of behavior related to place, advocating people presence on a twenty-four hour basis; lighting everywhere; no alcoves or passages that could hide potential muggers. Louis Mumford has criticized her recommendations, noting that she essentially is sacrificing all sorts of urban beauty in the name of safety. (Palen 1975:285)   We agree.   Recent stories of "Gypsy" pickpocketing, hustling, etc. from cities like Rome, Florence, and Venice would prompt the listener to want to stay at home. But, if these places were made safe through a kind of antiseptic planning would you want to visit them? Certainly the cultural ambiance would be lost.

Even Robert Martinson called attention to the place of incarceration becoming too much a "home" for young, chronic offenders.[3] He insisted that we somehow had to "...lure them out from being too comfortable." Unfortunately, Martinson could easily have been interpreted as calling for measures that would make them uncomfortable. It takes no real imagination as to how to accomplish such a goal. Lavrenti Beria-- that infamous director of Stalin's secret police-- was quoted in the late 40's as saying "... give me the man for one night, . . . in the morning I'll have him confess to being the King of England." Little imagination is needed to understand how behavior can be changed, provided we are willing to pay the price; and that price can be exorbitant for a civilized community.

Our own interpretation of Martinson is that he was referring to "drawing out" the incarcerated offender from his life style. . . his way of behaving. Martinson's audience was the vast number of practitioners and students in the correctional field. His message was to re-think the agenda of reform. Making the place of incarceration uncomfortable would be the least acceptable alternative.

Martinson, it will be recalled, published in 1974 the treatise that gave rise to the "nothing works" doctrine or agenda. And now in the 1990's we find the whole field of corrections plagued by the discordant advice and bickering from both the *left* and the *right*. The liberals (left) are seen as in a civil war, divided between trying to reaffirm the ideology of rehabilitation (Cullen/Gilbert 1982; Shireman/Reamer 1986; Miller 1989) and those calling for a "just deserts" approach to the offender population.(Fogel 1979; Singer 1979) These latter--sometimes called the justice model advocates-- insist that since nothing in rehabilitation has been "proven" to work, the actions of the justice system ought be to proceed in its response to crime and delinquency by adjusting "punishment to fit the crime." It should be pointed out that their liberal approach still remains somewhat intact by their insistence on the least possible *restrictive* response of justice to the individual. We are reminded here of a 1948 controversy in corrections where the late Donald Taft distinguished between offender *responsibility* and *accountability*. The conceptualization of responsibility was seen in moral/ethical terms while accountability would easily fit the current "just deserts" scheme of things.[4]

Those liberals still calling for a return to the rehabilitative model mostly argue that it was never truly implemented in the first place as the worst case against it, and that it "at least" had the compassion and humanism that is now lacking in their colleagues' call for "just deserts." This is not referred to as "best case" scenario,... perhaps only "better case."

These same old liberals are not as tolerant towards the conservatives who they infer have ulterior motives for wanting to get tough by abandoning rehabilitation. Taxes would be lessened as support for rehabilitation eroded. Government would be contracted. It is true that while a substantial number of liberals agree with the conservatives in abandoning rehabilitation and letting justice work itself out in a form of retributive justice, they differ on the quantitative side of punishment. Conservatives are interpreted as being "tough on offenders" as a means of deterrence or incapacitation. The former term is more general--deterring the offender OR others, while the latter term implies specificity: the offender will not offend while incapacitated--one way or another. Liberal justice model advocates call for the least restrictive interference in the lives of delinquents and criminals.

There is another "school of thought" so to speak, on how to best reform the offender. . . and the system. It could be looked upon as if on a continuum with the conservative justice model and rehabilitation. This is the radical perspective. Given some prominence--and respectability in the 1970's--radical criminology gained some limited momentum, particularly in the west (California) but elsewhere also. The radical perspective and agenda is that the whole justice system itself is too flawed, and we must abandon rehabilitation along with any "just deserts" model. (Krisberg/Austin 1978:105) What they would call for is no less than a total revamp of our entire social structure, particularly the economic part of it, which has as its core the distribution of worldly goods. Since we regard the radical agenda as unworkable at least at the present stages of civilized cultural happenings, we will not further address their writings here.

Viewing the current debate between the left (liberals) and the right (conservatives) over abandoning rehabilitation and establishing a justice model *vs.* returning to an ideology of rehabilitation, it seems prodigious to comment that the conservatives never appear to be satisfied unless left alone by government. Note the 1980's deregulation mania. The exception of course is in correctional practice; here conservatives call for interdiction . . . for others. But then again, liberals never seem satisfied leaving well enough alone. Note the 1960's plethora of social tinkering -- all in the name of rehabilitation and reform. The energetic expansion of all sorts of plans to rehabilitate offenders--sometimes quite dubious--was bound (on hindsight) to bring about the reaction and turmoil within the correctional system that we are now witnessing. But for all of this we still think that -- tongue in cheek-- the best characterization of conservatives and liberals is that the former never want to start while the latter never want to finish!! Another way of putting it is that the conservatives seem more adept at subtraction and division while the liberal *forte* appears to be in addition and multiplication!!

Quite another observation along the same line is the shared distrust in the institution of State, together with its associative governmental functionaries, by the conservative and the liberal "justice model advocates." Though differing in degree of mistrust, they are more aligned with the radical left in this regard. They differ from those older liberals still calling for a return to the values stressed in rehabilitation who seemingly have not lost their faith in a state social welfare system. Perhaps their faith is shaken a bit, but it is still there.

A perusal of the past several paragraphs and the reader will be forgiven for not knowing where *our* position on rehabilitation or just deserts stands. This is deliberate on our part. Serving careers in the Academic community one would find it difficult *not* to be liberal. It is not just by chance or prejudicial error that academicians are "suspect" of liberal tendencies by the press, ubiquitous masses, and public officials. Perhaps Peter Berger (1971) captured this enigma best when he wrote about the social scientists' penchant for calling attention to social problems; the bearer of ill tidings and all that such would entail.

Yet it is equally difficult for those of us in Academia who have had considerable experiences in the correction field to sit comfortable in a conference audience while our colleagues depict the unwholesome -- sometimes depraved-- functionaries of the correctional apparatus. Guards, attendants, clinicians, teachers and administrators alike in places of incarceration are so often vilified. A perusal of not only the popular press but also of the professional literature (Bortner 1982; Cullen and Gilbert 1982: Forward by Cressey) will confirm this.[5]

In this regard we would like to pose a sociological concept that we might call the *actor-role congruency fallacy*. Just as the ecological or aggregative fallacy correctly points out the inherent discrimination outcomes when the group (aggregate) is blamed for the deviant actions of the individual, (and *vice versa*) so also is a whole *role* blamed for the transgressions of (single) individuals -- and/or vice versa.

In terms of the ecological fallacy the Blacks in America are blamed for crime, welfare fraud, illegitimacy and similar social problems. The actor-role congruency fallacy would point out that whole roles (and statuses) that people sometimes act and occupy are blamed for individual transgressions. We then find police officials--wardens,guards and others being blamed for what has become anecdotal. "...that Red-neck Bull 'whatever-his-name was.'" Anyone acting in the role (past or present) is assumed to carry the debilitative baggage as part of their social repertoire.

Zimbardo's study with Yale College students where some played the part of guards and others played the part of prisoners was not only popular but was popularized to the extent that conclusions were drawn such that when one plays a societal role,...action is pre-ordained. (Babbie 1988:23-25) We submit that this is nonsense. Zimbardo's study is good in Introductory Sociology courses because it instructs in role theory. It is alarming though when such studies are extrapolated to conclude the depraved nature of any institutional role. More will be said about this in later chapters. We merely posit a concept -- the *actor-role congruency fallacy* -- to make a point. Persons are free to act in good conscience. Not *all* -- or even most -- of correctional workers are "bad" people any more so than all AFDC mothers drive Cadillacs.

In this monograph we wish to address several items, three to be exact. Hopefully the reader will be stimulated by our sometimes deliberately provocative observations.

First, we will try to propose some sort of "middle ground" for the present controversy between the "just deserts" justice model and the rehabilitation model. It will not be all inclusive -- all things to all men. Rather we see in the present confrontation between liberals -- old and new -- and conservatives that there must be some reconciliation. While the old liberals (rehabilitation model ideologists) wait for a "return of the pendulum" where their values and efforts will be reaffirmed, the just deserts model coalition of the new liberal left and solidified right (conservatives) is running away with the show. But the squabbling between the two groups on the positions they take has been going on for well over a decade[6]. Clearly, not only can some common grounds be found, but common ground must be found such that our efforts at confronting the social problem of youthful deviance *not* be squandered.

Second, in the beginning of this chapter we address urbanism as a life style -- a way of life. Some parts of that life have more holding power than other parts. Some parts mesh well -- others do not. Delinquency is seen as one of those parts that does not; while the role of juvenile delinquent may be satisfying to the individual occupant, it can be pictured as fragmenting in terms of our urban culture. Frankly speaking we would consider delinquency -- and deviance -- to be a reaction to urbanism, *albeit* a negative one. Although we do not intend to write a tightly knit monograph detailing experimentally the social scientific evidence for our case, if we did, then urbanism would be placed as the independent variable while the dependent variable would be delinquency.

We do not completely disparage the multitude of articles that are tightly woven, scientifically erudite, with findings such as the intake of sugar and its relation to delinquency, (Rodale 1969) or that height is also correlated. (Sheldon 1949) But if we can monitor sugar intake, what can we do about height? Here we are reminded of Pitirim Sorokin's criticism of American Sociology: that it had a bad case of "quanto-phrenia," implying an over-reliance on statistical technique to make our inferences.[7]

If such exact (and exacting) studies sometime appear trivial (and in the case of height, one could argue that something could be done about the *social perception* of height, e.g., social class)[8] full blown studies such as the Drift thesis of David Matza (1964) suffer from the kind of criticism attributed to Will Rogers around WWI. Rogers, when asked what could be done about the German Submarine menace replied: "Boil the Ocean!" When asked again as to how one might accomplish such a feat, Rogers punch line was ". . . that's an administrative decision. I've just given a policy recommendation." For Drift theory . . . how do we handle the "will to infraction" of young delinquents, or the sense of anxiety that attaches to crime/deviance/ delinquency? Incidentally and not withstanding, we consider Matza's monograph on juvenile delinquency to be one of the *very best* . . . for all of the others insights he had to offer.

Again, we intend to explore urbanism as a way of life involving delinquency as an unfortunate by-product. Urbanization --a different concept connoting a process of becoming citylike (citification)-- will be seen as urbanism's reciprocal. The two are tied together. The latter-- urbanization--is seen as the development and proliferation of things. The former--urbanism--is seen as social accommodation and developing life ways; in a sense urbanism is human coping.

Third, we intend to make several recommendation as to what could be done about delinquency. Two of these will be rather general. Indeed, we will set forth these few more basic generalizations in the next several pages. Usually recommendations are placed in final chapters, but it is our feeling that some may be stated early on in this monograph. As Robert Merton

(1961) once insisted, one of the properties of a social problem involves not only the sense of feeling that something *must* be done, but also that it *can* be done. We will keep this admonition of his in mind as we write.

Some more specific recommendations will be found in the content of this monograph. Many should be obvious and common sense. But then again, one writer described ". . . genius as common sense to an uncommon degree." Many practitioners in the field of corrections have already on their own adapted their professional behavior in the areas we address. They know and understand what we *think* we do. Readers unfamiliar with the day-to-day experiences of correctional practice will hopefully develop at the least a sense of *entente* (hearing dialogue) if not *detente* (*verstehende*, understanding). If this can be achieved, perhaps all of us, all those interested in the social problem of juvenile delinquency, can move forward in the difficult task of making things better in our world, our cities, and in our lives.

A book, an article, a monograph, . . . even a report *is* addressed to an audience. Cullen and Gilbert (1982) specifically target the old liberal camp and indicate their hope for a return of a united front to embrace the rehabilitative ideal that was so prominent in the early decades of this century . . . until the nineteen seventies. Other authors have not been so direct at naming an audience, but their messages -- and most times even their titles -- are suggestive, if not abundantly clear.

It is our intention and hope that this monograph and its messages will be read by one group in particular. This is that large number of persons who are actually engaged in social confrontation with delinquents. These are the "front line troops," so to speak in any "war"on a social problem. There have been in the past "wars on poverty" (the Johnson years of the '60's), and "wars on drugs" (the Reagan years of the '80's), numerous "wars"on crime as stated in the mass media. Most of the messages seemed aimed at a general population of citizens. When such messages are so directed -- general consumption -- it is our feeling that they become trivialized, often sensationalized, and in the process saturate the market place of ideas without adding much new. Those who work with delinquents are already sophisticated for this subject. We think we can offer additional insights for them.

College students, particularly at the sophomore and junior level, are in the formative stages of career development. Many of them begin to elect a lifetime, perhaps less in many individual cases, of involvement in the position of practitioner in corrections. They also are the intended audience here.

Perhaps some of our colleagues in the social and cultural sciences will also find this work interesting. We invite them to peruse these pages in the hope that they will be moved to make some use of our suggestions, which we are basing on our experience both in academia and practice. As will become apparent, our teaching colleagues are part of the equation where some solutions to the growing social problem of delinquency must be found. The college and University Professoriate is responsible for the education of past, present and future practitioners in corrections.

We do not have much more than a hope (and prayer) that others in the general public of American readers would be our audience. It must have been extremely satisfying for Professor George Gilder when his work on Trobriand Islanders was picked up by David Stockman[9] and made required reading for his staff at OMB during the early years of the Reagan administration. The Fourth Estate--the Press-- comments of the day on this event were that the conservative messages found in Gilder's work fit quite nicely with the then current thinking of this White House department. Most social scientists dream about the public policy implications of their writings, but few have little more than the hope of widespread readership where influence is perceived to occur.

This work is a monograph. In this we are following the advice of the late Professor Arnold Rose. (Stryker 1968) In commenting about the literature of sociology, Rose suggested that there were a profundity of professional articles being published where the reader was assumed to possess an abundance of knowledge on the addressed topic. Articles have become overly directed to a narrow audience because of this. In many instances it had become impossible to adequately peruse articles according to Rose.

On the other hand, Rose observed that the number and proliferation of textbooks were -- taken as a whole -- largely undifferentiated. Most any text looked like any other. They seem written "as if" the reader knew practically nothing. Every topic was laboriously illustrated. He was referring specifically to Sociology. We agree. In searching text books in corrections one would conclude that authors are mostly addressing an audience that knows practically nothing--or next to it--about the subject. Perhaps this is as it should be,...but why than do we have so many texts? A consequence is that we skim new texts in that tedious search for the one (perhaps) or few *new* ideas. Sometimes we are rewarded. A monograph by its very nature ought address a single topic; more sharpened and involved than the short article yet shorter and more to the subject than the text. The targeted audience is assumed to have some knowledge/interest beforehand, but long summaries and rehashing of writings found elsewhere is abandoned. Similarly, the form of erudite presentation of the article is avoided in the monograph.

As a final part of this introduction to our thoughts, we are setting forth two general recommendations as to what should or could be done in correctional practice to alleviate the social problem of juvenile delinquency. All of us who have taught courses in Criminology, Delinquency, Deviance and the like come to that point in our lives where we are asked, "What can be done?" The following brief paragraphs contain some of our more general ideas. We feel that implementation is possible, but yet, as can be seen, not without difficulty.

Our first recommendation has to do with the professional practitioners in corrections. These persons are mostly probation and parole officers, institutional staff, Agency workers and so forth. There is a great need to really, truly *professionalize*! Those working "in the field" (as the euphemism is stated) *must* become more closely identified, particularly among themselves, but also by the general public.

There is a litany of reasons why the "profession" is as it is today. David Matza (1964) correctly points out that correctional workers occupy a "quasi-profession," and that even clients of the practitioner see the "job" as not particularly worth-while. He compared it somewhat with other "quasi-professionals" in Teaching and Nursing, where similar ambivalent and negative public attitudes prevail.

Another of the more obvious reasons for the low esteem in professional corrections has to do with low pay. Any perusal of newly hired college graduates will show the monetary worth of the various professions. Such is true even when comparisons are made ten and twenty years later, when experience has been factored into the equation. Salaries are pitifully low. From the standpoint of good public policy, there is no excuse for this deplorable situation.

Some of the more subtle reasons have to do with a "kind of" patronage and nepotism. Qualifications for entry and promotion in the correctional profession have typically had more to do with a kind of politics and knowing the right parties than it has to do with credentials. Police " professionals" in particular have had their own terminology recognizing this. As Niederhoffer (1967) pointed out, the *Rabbi* was the reference name given to that person (the patron) to whom the job was owed. We have witnessed the identical situation in professional corrections. Political party affiliation, union membership, even ethnic and religious background often have meant more than experience and credentials; to speak of this, to raise it to consciousness, is, to say the very least, not polite in political circles.

We say a "kind of" patronage and nepotism holds for entry and advancement. Certainly this is not true in all -- perhaps even most -- cases. Though we are unsure as to its pervasiveness, what does hold true is that it adversely affects/influences the professional mystique. Political affiliation, family, even religion, and or neighborhood membership often became the *sine qua non* of the credential portfolio. Although it is believed that the older forms of patronage have dissipated somewhat, the vestiges of this past American political feature are still evident. One has only to follow the newsprint in contemporary America to come to this conclusion. Jacksonian political patrimony is alive and well in modern times.

Then there is the matter of credentialing itself. What should be the background preparation to the field of corrections? Much less than that which is desirable is settled for because there is "need to fill the positions." But in an analogous situation in the Teaching profession, should the correctional field be a kind of "proving grounds" where people decide where to make their careers? Keith Geiger (1990 President of the NEA) stated that he was " . . . not interested in people who go into teaching for three or four years until they grow up and see what they want to do in life."(*Newsweek* 7/16/90:63) Perhaps he was anticipating a situation which would undercut K-12 teaching careers through an influx of applicants for short term positions, and job applicants that possessed peripheral qualifications. Such a situation is endemic to corrections.

A final note on professionalization in corrections. Over the past several decades many Associations have been formed. Some are unions in the spirit of Trade and Craft. The correctional field should follow the example being set by the giant Teacher's unions. Efforts to have "dialogue" and accommodation with the AFT and NEA have been taking place. These two educational Associations (unions) have long been divided over turf, membership and other issues; some of their leadership see the benefits of a united front for the teaching profession. The correctional field should follow this example. They would have much to gain through regional and national consolidation.

Our second general recommendation has to do with the enterprise of Education. It ought to be easy (or easier, as the case may be) because many of the audience to which this monograph is aimed are professional educators -- the Professoriate.

Our recommendation here really is twofold: at the higher education level, educate to and for the profession; in Primary and secondary education, educate children--the young citizens--to living in a twenty-first century urban society.

The professoriate in University and college teaching has control over curricula, grades, book assignments and the whole gamut of academic work. They are not entirely consistent in exercising controls, but it is argued that *IF* they were, then credentialing in corrections would become a reality. The *vita*, the credential *resume*, would take on meaning.

In 1983 a simple and brief survey of Colleges of Education at two dozen Universities revealed that *none* actually taught teachers to teach in correctional facilities. We were not surprised because experience had taught us that teaching professionals in the institutional settings had come to their jobs by way of many routes -- none of which was professional preparation to work with the incarcerated delinquent. Yet correctional institution *programs* in education have for decades occupied a secure position among programs. At the very least the teachers were always paid more than the guards, social workers, intake workers or probation staff. Why then had not the credential mechanisms been put in force for an educational teaching specialty for corrections?[10]

Four decades ago the correctional field had many practitioners who had come to their jobs by way of very diverse educational preparation. Young college graduates with majors ranging from English to Philosophy, Theology, Psychology, Sociology, Law etc. were common. In 1990 we find the law degree still a major part of the credentials in some significant areas of correctional service. We are referring particularly to Parole/Probation work. This in itself would not be a "severe" problem, but for the most part the law school graduate usually occupies a place in the correctional field *until* his/her career in law practice is solidified. We are not referring to the Public Defenders office or the office of the Prosecutor where a law degree is the obvious credential. As Professor Robison (1960) has indicated, the position of Judge of the Juvenile Court also requires legal training; implicit with her observations though, would be a more substantial background in the humanities and social sciences.

Over the past few decades a large number of Criminal and Juvenile Justice programs have been initiated at many Universities. These are to be commended. We recommend their continuance and absorption into the academic mainstream. Those of us who are familiar with academic communities know how easily various programs, non-departmental "studies" and the like can be relegated to second class citizenship. This does not auger well for their graduates.

Perhaps teachers in primary and secondary education do not have as much control over the kinds of student academics as do the university professoriate. Yet their influence on America's youth is so important that it is almost trite to point it out. While pre-collegiate teachers have less to say about the academics, they have more than their proportionate share of input into the *activities* surrounding education. Primary and secondary school teachers are "closer" to their students.

What is needed is a new dedication to teach our young people to get along with each other in our modern western, industrialized and urban society. We need to teach civility. And this is *not* the emphasis in civic classes, history, social studies or any number of courses that are offered at the K-12 level.

We argue that it is the responsibility of the Educational system to teach values -- civility -- to our young people. If the Professoriate, the Colleges of Education, the various Boards of Education around the U.S. and the teacher Unions would come together and cooperate on a course of action as to what should be taught -- namely civility -- then it is our contention that something would be accomplished in diminishing the problems that we now face in corrections. The Professoriate and the Teachers Unions in particular have the organizational structures in place that would allow for cooperation in implementing teaching in civility by our K-12 teachers. This is where a start could be made. Singular voices of top teacher Union leaders should call for such action.

In the past several decades, K-12 teachers have been constrained to teach personal values. This probably represents a reaction to values as if they had a religious quality, and of course everyone knows that since Church and State are separate, religious teaching is out. But it can be argued that teaching civility and moral values transcends the teaching of formal religion. It is not supposed to be the same. Such teaching can be accomplished without reference to denomination, sect, or religious affiliation.

The Social studies teachers most times had the task of teaching watered down values of patriotism, citizenship, respect for the American flag, and the like. But since the social studies teachers also had the task of teaching self worth, self awareness, and similar newer ideas of educational practice, what went along with this was the teaching of a benevolent self-interest. Coupled to this was the notion of an enlightened despotism.

Benevolent self-interest was the idea that the self is very precious; that the self has only one go-around in this existence; that others should not be *used* if such could be avoided,... but, and this was most important, remember *Number One*! *Numero uno* became the time's catchword. An enlightened despotism was the idea that we should do good for others, whether they saw it that way or not. Others were to be helped, like it or not.

All of this became the antithesis of teaching civility. Good manners were thought to be either counterfeit or the veneer of the crackpot. Little wonder that much of the outcome of urban social relations has been delinquency, crime, and deviance of all sorts. It was, after all, the American theologian Reinhold Niebuhr (1966) who noted that self interest, however benevolent, is predatory at its roots!!

We want to end this chapter on a positive note. Practitioners in corrections can emulate and even transcend professional practice: they are teachers. Teachers in America can do what they ought, and that is to teach civility: for they are practitioners of an art that has its origin in antiquity. The essence of academic freedom is to teach what ought be taught.

In Chapter two the concerns of those within the correctional field are addressed. These are the actors, the supporting cast of parole/probation workers, custodial workers, attendants/guards, intake workers, police juvenile officers, and others who intersect the lives of urban delinquents. We even note the role of volunteer in corrections, which has become "so-so" prominent in recent years. Perhaps it is because they are obviously so diverse in their present positions, backgrounds and in their workplace tables of organization, ... it is difficult to write about them "as if" they were whole units, rather than an assortment of parts. We still believe there is more in common that is shared than there is divergent. Experience has taught us that at the practice/practical level of day-to-day interaction, a very wide variety of correctional roles interact, interface, communicate, and otherwise socialize.

It therefore behooves us to address these various roles, together with the similar problems that are encountered. All too often the confrontations between and among these roles are worked out in terms of the outcomes over distribution of the "perks" attached to incumbency: pay, position, prerogative, ... power.

ENDNOTES for CHAPTER ONE

1. An excellent review of the literature comparing the German and the Chicago (American) influence on Sociological thought is to be found in the first twenty-three pages (an Introduction) of Sennett's *Classic Essays on the Culture of Cities*. (1969)

2. The very early formulation of the classic viewpoint of human ecology by Burgess and Parks (1925) was their concentric zone hypothesis. This "place" oriented conception of human behavior was so pervasive that its influence was widely appreciated. A mid-1960 review of the U.S. secondary school Social Studies literature found zonal hypotheses present in *all* then current texts. In the 1950's Insurance company fraud investigators were schooled in the ramifications of place related arson, hi-jacking and other consumer crime. Until the mid to late 1980's, any teacher lecturing in Introductory Sociology courses would find that several students were already aware of Burgess' "concentric zone theory;" part of the reason for this must have been that the "theory" lends itself so well to the expository lecture. Secondary school teachers had opted for it because it was fascinating, easily taught, quickly learned, and above all, worthwhile in fashionable academe. All this has changed; current beginning College students have never heard of Burgess or his zonal theory. Contemporary sociological perspectives have finally caught up with mass society; ecology and zonal hypotheses have been down-played in sociological research for *several* decades.

3. Martinson did the audio/visual commentary for several instructional/documentary films. Two of these films: *Delinquency: The Chronic Offender* (also subtitled "Shot-Gun Joe"), and *Delinquency; Prevention and Treatment*, (BAVI; 1970 and 1976) provide an excellent insight into Martinson's thinking on the "nothing works" thesis.

While there is no mistake as to his evaluation and criticism of failed rehabilitative programs for the delinquency problem, it would appear equally true that Martinson would reject giving up on youthful offenders, as contemporary punishment and "just deserts" advocates seem to have done. What Martinson appears to opt for in these film presentations is the re-arrangement and re-alignment of the agenda for problem solving in Corrections.

4. Following World War II, Professor Taft was interested in the war crimes trials being conducted at Nuremberg.

While speaking against such adjudications, he seemed equally concerned with the old social controversy of affixing *cause* in the social sciences. He had become engaged in academic dispute concerning the concept of *individual responsibility*. In 1948 he told his students that it would be better to discard the notion of *responsibility* as a *moral*. Taft was indeed a *relativist* in the cultural and social sciences. He proposed employing the concept of *accountability* when-ever and where-ever individual *cause* was assessed.

5. It is interesting to note that some authors who early on had been so critical of the practitioners in the Correctional field now appear to be saying that the "good old days" of the rehabilitation heyday were not all as bad as were earlier depicted. Donald Cressey in his Forward to Cullen and Gilbert's work (1982) suggests this point.

6. The National Center on Institutions has held two impressive conferences on *Reaffirming Rehabilitation*, in 1986 and again in 1990. The only criticism of this effort is that the conferees and others in attendance appear all of a like mind (1990). Punishment and "just deserts" advocates were noticeable by their absence. The impression is like that of proselyting for Catholics in Ireland, or Democrats in Chicago's ethnic enclaves.

7. Sorokin had been openly critical of mathematical modeling in science during the 1950's and later; see especially the notes to chapter seven of Loomis and Loomis. (1965)

8. Persistent reference to height and physique as correlated to social class backgrounds--and delinquency--has been observed in the sociological literature.

9. Back in 1981 when President Reagan first took office, his appointee to the Office of Budget and Management, David Stockman, was constantly in the news for several months, culminating with a widespread news story where the interviewed Stockman was quoted as disagreeing with what was to become widely known as "Reaganomics" and "trickle down theory" of economic wealth distribution. Stockman was portrayed in the Press as a kind of boy wonder,... intelligent, decent, hardworking, and ambitious. It was in a *Newsweek* publication (*circa* 1981) that his admiration for the research of George Gilder was pointed out. Since that time Gilder has authored numerous columns of his own in various contemporary journals, including the Wall Street Journal.

10. Miss Wendy Volz completed an interesting and brief survey of Departments of Education at about two dozen U.S. Universities. The term paper that resulted from this effort was part of the requirement for a course in Juvenile Delinquency.(1983) The question addressed was the presence (or

absence) of teacher preparation for working and teaching in a correctional facility. We were surprised that *others* were surprised that, for all intent and purpose, such preparation was non-existent.

Anyone with institutional experience could confirm this observation. Miss Volz' paper received first recognition award at the 1983 Wisconsin Criminal Justice Education Association annual meeting. (Fall, 1983)

2
The Supporting Cast

When we address the various positions that people occupy in the Correctional apparatus, it is with the understanding that there are many roles with accompanying statuses that are apparent. A perusal of textbooks and the popular literature reveal a wide variety and hierarchy of positions, ranging at the "top" end to Juvenile Court Judge, on through police officer, probation/parole officer, attendant, guard, agency personnel (public and private), and various other categories of cook, kitchen worker, janitorial staff, secretary, and so forth. It is probably somewhere in the mystique of our cultural imperatives that assumption is made that only certain role performances are respectable and meaningful in the interaction that brings about the amendment of juvenile character. We have Goffman (1961) and later the popular novel/film of Kesey (*One Flew Over the Cuckoo's Nest*; 1962) for knowing better. Both drew attention to the total circle of players of any social situation. Though we should have known all along, all of the persons acting in roles that impact on a juvenile referred for service and help are significant; some roles have their significance in ways that are not immediately apparent. If there are doubts here, just ask some young person who has been through the system which people he or she remembers, which ones were important in the daily interaction. Or ask any former employee of the system. They will know; tables of staff organizational structure provide nothing more than "helpful hints."

From the very beginning of a police encounter -- which is the way it usually starts -- on through a Court appearance, perhaps to a custodial institution, there are many interactions with significant others. As adults of course, we understand that some encounters are more significant or meaningful than others. Some of the persons in the encounter process are Decision Makers affecting welfare and the future.

19

It is for this reason -- among others -- that the top Decision Maker in a Juvenile Court, the Judge, ought stand out. Judicial garb is one way of standing out. We were witness to many occasions where certain judges in Juvenile court proceedings have attempted to be more informal, more egalitarian, less involved with the trappings of judicial process. Attempts often were made to downplay the perception of social power attached to rank and position. We also have seen misunderstandings result when juveniles "attention to detail" were less on the Decision Makers actions and words and more on peripheral functionaries. Look at any Juvenile Court where the Judge stresses informality and you will find the most well dressed person to be the Bailiff. It becomes somewhat comic to witness a commitment to a training school where a juvenile simply wasn't paying attention to the appropriate interaction.

All of this is to say that there are many in the supporting cast of the drama that takes place with juveniles. For this reason we would like to shy away from any usual style, addressing this role/status or that one-- the judge, the teacher, the social worker, the attendant, the custodial worker, and on and on. Instead we will try to speak to considerations that are germaine and genuine to most all.

David Matza has noted that "... with the (possible) exception of judge, all of the offices that regularly oversee the conduct of juveniles share a single overriding characteristic. They are all marginal professions. Teaching, social work, probation and law enforcement are all aspirant professions . . ." (1964:144) Even though there are ubiquitous claims to professionalization through attendance at seminars, workshops, staff meetings, University classes, membership in local, state, and national associations, the claims always appear as the suitor of an unrequited Love. And this is sad. These persons acting in their roles and jobs can and do perform for the most part efficiently and appropriately. It is not that they should stop promoting intellectual and social growth; but pursuing a goal that has really eluded them for so many decades only pulls away from those others with whom they share an on going commitment: to work with and service the social problem of juvenile misconduct.

Professionalization, again as Matza has noted "... derive(s) respect from the performance of tasks that are publicly acknowledged as vital and difficult, from their publicly acknowledged high social standing as manifested in high salary or prestige . . ." (1964:144) For many of the roles that are performed in the juvenile justice system, professional status was never a consideration. Unionization was seemingly sufficient for a large number of supporting staff and workers. One would have to wonder at some

Administrative efforts on the part of the authority structure in institutions and agencies, to "clone" professionalization for guards, police, case workers and even office personnel. The notion is promulgated that if they are professional, there is no use or need for union organization. Is this merely a distraction?

In the last decade or so some unionization has taken the place of "professional organizations." This has been the case in several major Juvenile courts. There are Probation Officer unions. Though it is too early to see how effective they are becoming, unionization as an alternative to professionalization seems firmly established; this is not-with-standing the observation that many problems exist for these Associations in their interaction with "management." One would hope that in the 1990's this early stage of unionization becomes solidified. We are not sure it will or would do so under the guise of professionalization.

Teacher Unions have been far more entrenched in the United States. This has been the case not only for the K-12 persons in most of the school districts, it has also been the case for academic, technical, shop and craft teachers at juvenile correctional institutions. This is one source of friction in such institution: the so-called professional staff of social workers, counselors, and intake workers (those whose credentials call for the college degree) are more often than not paid less than unionized teachers working in the same place.

At these same juvenile institutions, and the courts, you will observe unionized workers from the crafts (electrical, plumbing, painting, stationary engineering and so forth) on a higher rung of the prestige ladder than the so-called professionals. The former are paid more; and there is a tug of war between the groups. Verbal sparring, veiled forms of "one-upmanship," is part of the daily routine. Most of the time it is covertly hidden below the surface of outsider recognition, but it is there none-the-less.

To be sure, many of the unionized jobs whose roles and positions interface with the social workers and their salaried peers are not paid more nor do they have more apparent prestige. The custodial staff --guards janitors, kitchen help and more-- are among the less well economically remunerated within both the correctional system and the union family itself. Politics such as it is in the United States has many public institutions where patronage is the model whereby jobs are filled. The Jacksonian ideal that the spoils of political contest go to the winner of public office persists. And this means that many of the lower paid union jobs at public institutions have been traded off, *quid pro quo* by public officials to and from union officialdom.

As more and more of the marginal professions (Matza 1964) opt for unionization, and we do believe this will be the case, perhaps unionization will become more respectable. It is not difficult to understand and be aware of the fact that the 1980's was a poor period for labor organization. As indicated in chapter one, internal union squabbling as well as external 'busting' has been a plague for organizational efforts. In terms of the external threat to organizations, we would wonder to what extent administrators at public institutions have employed the services of management's union 'busting' services, techniques and hired-hand agencies. More will be said of this later.

Ken Wooden has written about "...what the penal trade refers to as the 'three empire system.' Made up of (1) guards and other custodial workers, (2) teachers, and (3) caseworkers, each group is different in scope and totally separated from the others." (1970: 14) Although he correctly identified a rather fascinating part of correctional institutional society and culture, we would like to expand on this.

A correctional institution is a total living place. Most present day institutions have given up on requiring staff to live on the premises. One of the current exceptions is the large facility for adult offenders at San Quentin, just north of San Francisco. Early on in this century both public and private correction facilities had live in staff. The then current thinking was that it was "cheaper," getting staff for much more than the forty plus hours a week. A half century-plus later found the experience wanting. Not only was staff burn-out too high a price to pay, but also the architects and builders were quick to point out the high dollar cost of institutional space. Some private places still hold on to some of these "models of living arrangements." We would prefer to think resident status for employees was only a temporary, *albeit* lengthy, failed experiment.

Notwithstanding whether staff live-in or not, correctional institutions are total, they are a total environment. There is an indigenous social structure and culture. One of the authors of this monograph lived and worked in a juvenile correctional institution for eight-plus years in the 1950's-60's, and when first entering that world-apart was told by an old friend Parole Chief that "...you're not changing jobs, you now have a position."[1] It wasn't too many years before understanding took place. The sociologist would say that total role commitment and socialization to different sets of normative structures evolved.

A recent visit to San Quentin's Yard where large numbers of inmates were recreating offers an interesting example. When asked why about a dozen inmates appeared to be separate from the rest of the population, more-or-less occupying an area where others did not go, the guard-escort commented that "...that's Indian (American) territory. That's their Holy ground. No one else goes there."[2]

We suppose that other places have their own culture. All of the three authors are from the current college campus. One time when one of the authors was having coffee and a chat with a rather perceptive student at the Campus Union cafeteria, the student pointed out the various tables and groups of students. Some were the greeks (fraternities), some were the soldiers (R.O.T.C.), while still others were pointed out as jocks (athletes) and still others, the "freaks" (student dissenters). Since this occurrence was over a decade ago,... the names probably have changed.

So we do indicate that institutional living has its own culture and is total.[3] In the next chapter we will want to again explore some of the ramifications present for this fact. Much can be made of this that is positive and worthwhile. On the other hand, we know all too well of the debilitating effect of incarceration. The last several decades have been witness to a plethora of writings pointing this out.

While Wooden described the Empire system in terms of three sets of role-types, essentially social workers, teachers and guards, the more astute observer of institutional life would note at least two other important "Empires." Namely, the administrators, on the one hand, and all those other staff in support roles -- the kitchen staff, the office personnel, sick bay, janitorial and so forth. If you were to visit an institution it is possible and perhaps even probable that someone would explain to you the "table of organization." Mostly these tables, usually charts of some variation, depict the various jobs/positions in a kind of hierarchy which would show authority and responsibility on a vertical axis; some jobs would be arranged on a horizontal axis to show similarity of role, prestige and supposed responsibility. Our point here is to advise *not* to take these too seriously if you are trying to find out how the system works in terms of overall stated goals. If the goal as stated by an institution was to rehabilitate delinquents, these tables would be of little service. However, if you wanted to identify various groups-- Wooden's Empires -- these tables would give some broad "hints." Without them it might take a long while, for instance, to realize that there were several part-time physicians, a full-time dentist and so forth. All of these jobs are involved in interaction with detained youth. We should be careful, as Kesey (1962) and Goffman (1961) were, to realize that even though some jobs/positions have as their primary reason for existence, the care, teaching and rehabilitation of others, many positions also have serious impact, in some cases profound.

Thus far we have spent more time addressing the 'total' institution than we had intended. This is probably because at these places life is condensed, so to speak. We can observe life 'wholestically'. The early Chicago School of Sociology (in Louis Wirth's time) was consistently interested in wholestic units of analysis. For the most part they concentrated on the concept of community, whether that community was the slum, the gold coast, the ghetto, or even some small town like Muncie or Bloomington, Indiana; New Haven, Connecticut; Matoon or Morris, Illinois.

It was only later that other whole living communities were addressed -- Nursing homes, prisons and the like. In the case of prisons, some of our more poignant insights have come from modern American literature, like for instance Truman Capote's film classic *"The Glass House."* (1974) This was a very emotionally wrenching depiction of a maximum security prison. In the case of Nursing Homes, a whole new sub-discipline of social gerontology has emerged. A Study by Jaber Gubrium (1975) is an in-depth look at a nursing home in Milwaukee. The analysis is strongly familiar, with findings suggestive of various empires of positions, role performances with elderly clients that conform to Goffman's model of institution: the closer and more informal normative relationships are to the client, the more important/relevant they become.

While total institutions offer a fascinating opportunity for analysis of wholistic systems of social intercourse, they are perhaps only the most visible and obvious. Not less important are the agencies, courts, half-way houses, shelters, community based centers and the like. They too have their 'empires.' While one training school in Illinois (St. Charles) had the 'insiders' knowledge of an institutional culture that portrayed the top administrators as "Father, Son, and Holy Ghost" (Superintendent, Intake Director, Cottage Life Director), ...the Juvenile Court to Chicago's insiders spoke of a "Catholic Judge, Protestant Chief, and Jewish Deputy." Most of these particulars have changed. One would wonder about their replacement symbols. What new imperatives to power are operative? What jargons are employed?

To be sure, there are differences in the public and private sectors, both at the institutional and agency levels. Two ambivalent themes in corrections for the past decade-plus (middle 1970's to present) have been de-institutiona-lization and privatization. The first has been the closing down and regrouping of resources for community based programs. Little did those who were the prime-movers at the beginnings of de-institutionalization factor-in the net-widening that would occur. More, not fewer, clients were brought into the system.

Privatization will continue through the 90's, but it is predicted that there will be a reversal in de-institutionalization; this has already happened at the adult levels in Corrections. Whereas Prison inmate populations were cut back a decade ago, they are currently bursting at the seams: Society doesn't seem able to build new prisons quickly enough.

We will address privatization again in Chapter Three. Advocates for this note the good things that will result from private management: accountability, dollar savings, bureaucratic tightening and other assets based on a kind of Business Model. It is surprising that the notion of a Business Model has not taken hold, like the notion of the Medical Model did in Corrections. One cannot attend a conference on corrections without hearing someone invoking the Medical Model in explanations of what's going on. Not so --as yet-- any reference to a Business Model. Critics of privatization, not particularly discounting accountability as a management technique, do wonder about responsibility in terms of ethical, legal and common sense standards. Shireman and Reamer label privitization "entrepreneurial corrections" (1986: 160), and we think this is most fitting in its pejorative subtlety.

One recommendation that has come out of the Correctional literature (Cullen and Gilbert 1982: 275), is for the creation of a type of ombudsman position within (perhaps outside of?) the system. The reader of urban studies literature will recognize the role, job, position of ombudsman. Classical European cities often had some person who was not *in* or *of* the bureaucracy, not (supposedly) beholden to the power elites, who could be the conduit on an avenue of redress. If and when problems arose within city government between the bureaucratic functionaries and the people, affected persons could go directly to the ombudsman for help. This person had the authority and power to circumvent what we know of in our culture as "red tape." The job of ombudsman would be something like a hybrid of our "whistle blower," and a director from the Environmental Protection Agency. Unfortunately, either American culture is so different in this particular aspect from European city development and culture that we don't truly understand the role of ombudsman, or it is an anachronism that only is useful as an ideal type, not be realized in real life.

In terms of the correctional situation, the ombudsman as portrayed in the literature would be re-active to problems. Very few of the writers urge a pro-active type of role for an ombudsman. Our own thinking is that institutional roles can and should address the problems better, and agencies should be set up similar to Environmental Protection and Economic Opportunity of the Federal government. Problems to be solved ought not to have to wait until they become truly catastrophic. Pro-activism would require more time and effort being spent by the providers of correctional service. Particularly where public funds are allocated for private carriers of any type of program, venture or simply, for incapacitation of offenders; some type of oversight ought to occur before getting started. Too often this is overlooked in favor of *post hoc* evaluation, after the monies have been spent. We should know not only what any program or effort will purport to accomplish, we should know (and screen) those who will be involved.

One criticism of privatization of correctional services is that management, in hiring for those low level jobs, will have to ignore serious credentialing problems of employees because of lowered pay. Such cannot be allowed to happen. But we cannot and should not wait for a serious problem to be reported/dealt with by an Ombudsman or other vigilante person or committee.

Under the public sector system where institutions are run by public employees, levels of authority and responsibility can be clearly drawn. Under the privatization process, the "hired hand" can be fired, but the stake in career is never as clearly evident as it is in the public sector. Career people have a continuing and clear vested interest in not being fired from the position.

Another recommendation that has come out of the literature for corrections is a calling for people to work in the field who are advocates for juveniles. This is not entirely new. The notion that the Probation Officer, even though an Officer of the Court, was kind of *amicus curiae* (friend of the Court), looking to the interests of juveniles has been with us for decades. During the rehabilitative heyday of the first half of this century, Probation staff most always 'tilted' in favor of accused juveniles in court hearings. This only changed after the nothing works thesis became entrenched, and the just deserts agenda took hold following the mid-1970's. (Cullen and Gilbert 1882: Chapter 7; Shireman and Reamer 1986: Chapter 7).

What is somewhat new in the call for child advocates is that the correctional enterprise engage the non-traditional employees, ...those that are not the "nine-to-fivers." To a certain extent the non-traditionals have always been around. (Shireman and Reamer 1986: 167-172). And anyone who has been a Field Parole/Probation Officer knows that his job ethic doesn't resemble the traditional American value of forty-hours a week. Clifford Shaw's field workers at the Chicago Area Project were some of the most non-traditional street workers one would encounter (Snodgrass 1982).[5]

But what we think is really new is a calling for a process to somehow formalize (institutionalize) the type. We would urge caution here. Career orientation and advancement in positions have always followed the typically American work ethic: Work hard, keep your nose to the grindstone and you will be rewarded. Critics inveigh what has become anecdotal, citing the "Peter principle", ...that promotions occur to the level of incompetency of the promoted. Public employers such as teachers, hospital and correctional positions are particularly vulnerable to such criticism. Such is preposterous. The evidence that is cited is purely anecdotal, like those used to portray welfare fraud with stories of welfare mothers driving Cadillacs, or widespread use of food stamps to purchase liquor and cigarettes.

We would caution against tampering with institutional roles such that the rewards are further diluted. Pointing to job satisfaction, personal accomplishment and psychological fulfillment may be worthy for its own sake, but it will not replace career advancement which will and should be coupled with monetary considerations. We are suspicious of those who preach that financial rewards attached to careers are all peripheral. The Conflict theorists have performed a noteworthy service in pointing out that it is in the interest of those in power and authority to downplay rewards for career advancement that result in higher cost.

Another reason we would urge caution in concentrating on the creation of positions for the corrective system that are not the "nine-to-fiver's,"is that they often appear to be particular personality types. Often eschewing convention, family, and even health concerns they can be unpredictable. Any agency, institution, court or field office has bureaucratic needs that must be met.

We are reminded of that film "Lawrence of Arabia," where the protagonist was able to lead an immensely successful army of divided Bedouin Tribesmen across desert hardships to finally take the fortified city of Aquaba. Aquaba, defended by the Turks in World War I never anticipated an assault from behind and had stationed its cannon pointing to the sea; they couldn't be turned around. But when Lawrence finally occupied the city, all of his skills of leadership were to no avail in running the day-to-day operations that had to go on. Water, electricity, sewage, all of the City's infrastructure ceased to work.

Another example and reason to be cautious of any quick rush to bring in and institutionalize the role of the "not nine-to-fiver" can be found in Union organizational literature. The day-to-day operations have the ordinary leadership roles in place. The usual daily operations are carried out by men and women who clearly separate their work from the rest of their lives. But when there is a real confrontation with management, different leadership takes over. Different people and types are called upon. Perhaps this is why outside consulting firms have profited in recent years. There is a recognition that others must be in charge to do the unconventional. But their roles can hardly be formalized into the ongoing process.

A way around the problem by getting the best of both worlds, having unconventional thinking and acting, together with institutional roles and careers within corrections would be to rely more on duality of careers. The women's movement or whatever it has been called, that has drawn attention to the female population in the last decade-plus has pointed out an immense amount of untapped resources. Homemakers who have had their careers truncated because of early personal choice for family and children would appear to be an obvious source of persons for careers in corrections. This is already happening, as any college professor in sociology knows. They are returning to careers that here-to-fore were not possible. What is needed now is change in the American ethic of work. Employers still are suspicious of employment where their demand for total commitment to job appears challenged. Personnel policies need to be implemented that would account for longevity, experience, retirement, and promotion. Because of Nursing shortages, the health care fields are already accommodating to their problems in many of the ways that we would envision as applicable to corrections.

Quite another type of "dual career" that would be useful in corrections would be the employment of student help, particularly at Institutional settings. Boys Town in Nebraska had University students employed as live-in cottage supervisors. We know of other institutional settings that employed college students where this has been practiced. Arden Shore, a private institution north of Chicago on the shores of Lake Michigan was one. Very often the problems of scheduling are a "nightmare" often leading administrations to forget the whole deal and return to hiring people who can be "counted upon" in time schedules. This is too bad in a way, because the loss of aspirant workers for the system can be more debilitating than the scheduling dilemmas. And since one of the authors of the monograph has had near nine years experience with "scheduling dilemmas," we speak from experience. It would be better for institutional operations to hire more qualified and credentialed employees. A strong case can be made that upper classmen at Universities and Colleges, while lacking the baccalaureate, possess a kind of minimal qualification. This is especially true for students majoring in any of the social sciences. They certainly possess more coping strengths to interact with young delinquents than do persons hired without too much regard for any formal academic background.

The role of the volunteer in Corrections has been around for a long time. Organizational efforts have been more recent, like that under the sponsorship of the National Association of Volunteers in Criminal Justice. Initially it was associated with religious and philanthropic groups, and generally under the auspice of some church denomination, veteran group and/or even community organization. It is probably rare that individuals on their own behalf could volunteer and gain access to actually performing volunteer service. Occasionally, individuals appear, volunteering their time, experience and expertise. On their own, they are quite often suspect by administrators. This is undoubtedly the case because of the difficulty in checking into the background of some persons. Any administrator of a correctional enterprise, whether it be an agency, institution or whatever has the "horror story" that can be referred to for individual volunteers, and even some that have had the sponsorship of worthwhile groups.

But the "horror stories" are not confined to volunteers; even hired staff can and sometimes do become involved in absolutely ludicrous behavior. From the administrative standpoint though, it is more rare, and on the occasion that it does occur they have, at least, the dubious discomfort of knowing that at least it was their own fault. Within memory, it was our most shocking discomfort to know of an institutional adult employee's attempt to bite a boy's nose off during an unfortunate encounter that should have been handled differently -- to say the very least. Even though the employee was forthrightly dismissed from employment, the administration was left with the problem. How is such an injury to be explained to parents, guardians and others? Needless to say, the incident provided the impetus for a tightening up of policy reflected in the hiring process.

When volunteers become involved in anything approaching such an indiscretion, their auspice group is or can/should be called into account. It takes no imaginative leap to see and understand the difficulties encountered when two administrative groups must "lock horns," so to speak. All too often, the protection of agency or institution prestige is set above common sense.

Volunteerism has grown much in the last decade or so. The 1980's saw a widening of this social activity. Even earlier, during the Kennedy years, there was the introduction of the Peace Corps and its domestic counterparts, like VISTA. But these were different. They were more full time. And the people volunteering were getting something tangible in return; this in no way diminishes their worthwhile and humanistic service. But there was some remuneration, and their credential portfolios were enhanced. It might very well be profitable for the correctional enterprise to follow these earlier leads, like the Peace Corps and establish inner city, urban 'volunteer' programs. We do not see these as similar or dissimilar to the aforementioned 'nine-to-fivers' debate that we addressed. It is different. For one thing the Peace Corps volunteers were for specified time periods, and were much more akin to our present internship programs that have proliferated in university teaching. The 'real' difference is that college interns get (only) coursework credits. We would envision paid activity. Such activities are programs that would have to be initiated at the Federal level -- like in the Kennedy/Johnson years. At present we do not see this as forthcoming, although the merits and implications for social problem solving seem indisputable.

As volunteerism grows and becomes an ubiquitous part of Correctional activity, we would caution that it should be limited, selective, and totally supervised. This is not the case now. And we do recognize and 'tip our hat' to those who now occupy positions as Volunteer Coordinator for many of the agencies, Courts, institutions and the like. They do not have an easy job.

In the years to come the population of potential volunteers will become much larger. Demographics, the advent of early retirements, and the continued good health of many of our elderly citizens will see to that. There will also be many additional years of worthwhile fellow services that will be available by way of an aging, yet productive, population. The need is there and this need can and should be matched up with calls for genuine contributions to society. This can be done but caution must be taken so that the appearances of meaninglessness, or worse, sham, takes hold, and all sorts of volunteers and potentials return to television and other casual pastimes.

We are particularly concerned that the overriding message of volunteerism does not turn out to be a conservative ideology that taxes will thus be lowered, or that social welfare will be changed to handle the concomitant social problems through greater reliance on this source. The matter of fact is that volunteers do save money, monies that would otherwise be spent on staffing salaries, private hired hands, and even in many instances on equipment resources. Volunteers not only give of their time; many volunteer their own private resources as well. Note for instance the use of personal autos by volunteers. But if this message of "money saved" comes through loud and clear,... can cynicism be far behind? Volunteers and potentials will quickly know if and when they are being used.

It is not enough simply to have a volunteer program. The services of volunteers ought be meaningful. It ought not and cannot be viewed as a kind of therapy for the giver (the volunteer) any more than it is viewed as something that an agency, court or institution ought to have, ...simply because its the "in thing" to do. On the other hand, if volunteerism is a 'two-way street', volunteers AND clients both benefit! (We don't have an English word like volunteer, do we?) If this is not part of the scheme then one would have to wonder what is going on! Therefore, we repeat that volunteer activities should be limited, selective, and totally supervised. It would not hurt at all, too, to have periodic assessments; to evaluate the services. This is one reason we are uneasy at too much reliance on volunteer activities. There ought to be no *responsibility* discount because no ones's getting paid!

J. Sterling Livingston, former Dean of Harvard's Business School, has pointed out a management style in the United States that he referred to as "management by exception." (Ziff-Davis Pub. Co., 1974) By this he meant that supervision of employees was always based on negative practices, ... searching out, looking for those parts of the job that were still left undone or lacking in some way. It is a critical and criticizing approach. He has urged managers to be what he called a "positive Pygmalion," complimentary toward workers, always trying to emphasize their strengths rather than weaknesses. (The Pygmalion effect in Sociology has to do with the self-fulfilling prophecy; persons act as they are treated.) Even though it is rare to find administrators and others in managerial positions in the Correctional field that possess formal training and/or degrees in Business Administration (or related training), most of them do appear to have internalized the "management by exception" technique described by Professor Livingston. In courts, agencies, and institutions alike there is often an Administrative penchant for making it "hard" on the staff. It seems that the conclusion is often drawn that if the guards, social workers, teachers and others are "edgy,"...everything must be going well. The opposite implication is thus imputed that something must be wrong when staff morale is really high and they appear to be enjoying their jobs. The real paradox here is that Administrations also cater to the *caveat* that they must portray a work place free of internal strife, possessing high morale and teamwork as the guiding policy. It is left unquestioned that their own management style is responsible for many of the problems that result in such negative situations. Little wonder that cynicism among the staff results.

One could perhaps understand the historical background and setting of American business and industry that led to this unfortunate practice of management by exception. But for the most part, Administrators in the Corrections field have usually had extensive training in the social and behavioral sciences. The point is not lost on staff that the positive Pygmalion approach is urged as policy in treating clients and inmates, and yet denied to them in their own work situations.

Judges in particular need to be aware of the positive Pygmalion concept and the notion that management by exception is part of the American scene. Former Judge Sophia Robison notes a typology of Juvenile Court Judges and pointed out that one of her observed Judge-types was that of the *Antagonist.*(1960: 251) The Antagonist Judge apparently views his role to be one of hostility toward all those with whom he comes in contact. We have known such types. Their only seeming consistency is that they treat clients in adjudication as well as staff equally critically and with hostility. Fortunately, not all 'types' of judges are like this, as even Judge Robison noted. Since Judges' formal training is far and wide from the legal standpoint, the Law Schools, we have urged a greater infusion of the social and behavioral sciences there. It is not enough just to have some undergraduate courses that are in the social sciences for pre-law. The legal persons have one of the few real and substantive claims on what can be called a Profession (Matza 1964: 144). One way to implement a greater infusion of the social sciences into the legal system is for the Professoriate -- college and university Professors -- to urge their undergraduates in Sociology, Psychology, Social Work and other disciplines to look to post-graduate work in the Law. This has been happening to a certain extent in recent years, but it is still far too limited.

Since our form of government in the United States is composed of three (separate) branches of the executive (administrative), legislative, and judiciary most citizens have the notion that the judicial is really separate. We have been taught from childhood that there are these three and that while there are checks and balances between them, they still remain separate. Such abstraction of function is more often to be found in a kind of 'ideal' rather than reality. Many, many times the Judge finds that he is the one in charge of what is going on in a Court. He is the Chief Executive Officer. An old story that would often play around Juvenile Courts was that a new Judge would be treated with condescension by social work staff, viewing his role (both by him and staff) as a mere "rubber stamp." This all changed when the Judge suddenly realized that nothing happened without his signature. His importance was established. Money did not move, anywhere, without his signature.

While it has always been the case that Judges were in charge of administrative detail, trained as they were in the law they seemed to prefer to have others do that work on their behalf. For Juvenile Courts this has always been where the *hiatus* between law and Social/Behavioral Sciences occurred. Judges picked these "social work" types for administrative promotions. The most obvious was the position of Referee; this was usually an experienced social worker probation officer who acted on the Judge's behalf. Clients for the most part would conclude that the Referee *was* the Judge. The marriage of the two disciplines was always uneasy. Their formal training was different. In many ways it was as if they spoke different languages. Judges have in the past and still refer to the entire gamut of social and behavioral disciplines as "Social Workers." We have observed new Judges, mostly in the larger jurisdictions, not being able to differentiate agency staff from their own. Sometimes the outcomes are nothing less than hysterical or hilarious.

Some very recent happenings on the judicial scene make it more imperative for better understandings between the legal profession and the behavioral/social science practitioners. We are all aware of the controversy over "Bussing" in the United States. The Coleman report of the 1950's had a suggestion for the betterment of integrated black and white communities in the United States. Since *de facto* segregation was the reality in urban neighborhoods, the *future* could be more integrated neighborhoods *IF* school children were co-mingled across the school districts. The Courts ordered that school districts intermix children from racially segregated neighborhoods and places. When School Districts hesitated, balked, or were slow to respond to Court orders, many Districts were placed under the direct administrative control of a Judge. It was as if they had become bankrupt. We will not argue the merits or de-merits of these cases here. We only wish to point out that the Judge's role as administrator took a quantum leap.

In the last decade we have seen something new for the juvenile court. As we indicated previously, Judges ordinarily had left the administrative detail for others to handle. Perhaps it was the advent of bussing in the United States that brought to consciousness an awareness on the part of the judiciary that they could become more directly involved. In the mid-1980's, one of the judges in Wisconsin essentially declared by Court order that the handling of Juveniles was bankrupt.[6] He began to directly set the rules that in the past had been the prerogative of social service. This had the effect of controlling the outcomes, goals and activities of the social service practitioners. Undoubtedly more of this Judicial activity will take place. Opponents of this type of judicial activism are many, so we do not know as yet the conclusions, whether this will bode well for child care or not. In a very general way the "social workers" don't appreciate Judges interfering --as they think and say-- in what the behavioral/social science practitioners have long regarded as their own preserve.

We touched briefly on careers in the correctional field. During the last two decades new majors have been added to the curricula of many colleges and Universities that have been called -- among other names -- Juvenile and/or Criminal Justice. Whole Departments and even Schools within academia are now visible. Graduates from these places with this type of training credentials are first place in the job market within corrections. Time was when a degree from an accredited School of Social Work was first place; in Corrections (up until the advent of the Justice programs) almost any college degree sufficed, *albeit* in second place.

Often young college students seeking advice on the career opportunities within corrections ask about the potential. Usually their questions are rather general. They don't often ask what course, courses, or sequence ought be pursued. Serious aspirants can often be identified by simply asking them whether they want to work with people or things. We had a Public Defender as guest speaker to a class in Juvenile Delinquency recently. He was all prepared to give them an inspired lecture on his office and its importance to delinquency prevention and control. Then, before beginning, he asked the class "How many are going to be social workers?" Not one positive response followed. The Public Defender appeared shocked, and it was our guess that he was going to somehow change and/or dilute his prepared lecture towards generalities that would be more common in speeches elsewhere. We asked that he rephrase his question to "How many were aiming toward careers working with young people?" The positive student response approached one-hundred percent; the guest lecturer, satisfied, proceeded to address the class as planned.

Several observations can be made of this. First, as we indicated, we can tell something about an aspirant to the field of corrections by asking them about the types of persons they want to be working with as they follow careers; it is especially useful to know if they want to work with people at all. It is much too much to expect specifics. Few among us do not change goals on our way to career stability. More often it is several times. Second, our earlier observation that the legal profession seems to label all those who work with juveniles as "social workers." We do suppose that teaching and teachers must be an exception. A third observation, and one that is disquieting, is that No student (in a class of about three dozen) had indicated majoring in Social Work. On that campus there is an undergraduate Department of Social Work offering a baccalaureate program. We have Paul Tappan to thank for an insight to the answer of this apparent dilemma. (Robison 1960) Tappan had very early on noted that Social Work was more interested in the willing client; clients in delinquency are most often compelled to be involved. While we think there are significant changes for the social work practitioner, both in the formal preparation for entry into the field and in actual community practice, there does not appear to be a large number from social work that opt for Corrections.

It is not easy to advise young people as they decide about careers in the Correctional field. Its not an easy field in which to work and develop a career. Are there those among us --the policeman, the correctional worker, the teacher-- who have been secretly relieved that our children haven't followed in our footsteps? It is kind of like having our hearts swell with patriotism when reading reports of particular valor in military combat,...and yet being relieved that our sons didn't enlist in the Marines!

So what do we tell them, the would-be future probation officers, counselors, teachers...? In trying to be honest and straightforward, it must be pointed out that the pay is low; lower significantly than it is for most fields in which the college student could major. But then again, the interesting work they could be doing!! You can promise excitement!

We know the pay is low in Corrections. Some few in their careers make it to the top where "reasonable" pay prevails. Even there, though, compared to other disciplines the pay is remarkably low. We would only hope that pay as it is in Corrections does not become lower and more disproportionate from other disciplines. This is one reason, and only one, that we further urge unionization in Corrections. We are suspicious also of the call for privatization of services within Corrections, as has been the call for privatization of public schools. It appears now that privatization, along with de-institutionalization, are "code-words" by the Conservative politicians who want to cut taxes and become fiscally solvent by a contraction of the work force. Where most of the money goes in Corrections is human service, so any cutting will adversely affect humans, not equipment. The savings would be lowered salaries under privatization.

Another guest lecturer was recently speaking in a different class studying delinquency. She had been a former student of the Professor from the early 70's, but now is a supervising probation officer in a medium sized mid-western city.[7] At the Question and Answer time a young man in the back of the room asked "What was the best course she took at this University?" After a few moments of thoughtful reflection she responded: "English! the writing courses." Having thought about this for a while now, we cannot but affirm her observation. What she was saying was that the road to career advancement was through writing ability, to communicate, and to do it well.

Along with being able to communicate well in writing, persons working in Corrections have all been exposed to the concept of rapport. Basically it means the establishment of a genuine understanding relationship between two persons. As it is used, it conveys the meaning of a social service practitioner being responsible for augmenting this desirable relationship. But how does it come about? Is knowing the concept enough to implement it?

What happens to the establishing of rapport for instance, when a Probation Officer, or other practitioner interviews a delinquent (un-adjudicated) accused of rape? On the one hand David Matza introduced the concept of the ideology of child welfare, a kind of "Social Work ethic," which he believes is a further inducement for a young person to "drift" into delinquency. As Matza sees it, in the development of rapport, and not wanting to shut the relationship down, an interviewer in such a situation "tilts" towards helping the client develop socially acceptable reasons (excuses) for his behavior. This is similar to the psychiatric concept of rationalization But in psychoanalysis, rationalization is entirely individualistic: for the social work ethic there is a helper, a kind of conspirator.

It is easy enough to see where most interviewers can get caught in the above type of case. "After all," the interviewer might internally rationalize, "if I hinted at my true thoughts and feelings, he'd clam up and rapport is over."

We do believe there is an out here, but we leave it to be developed by our teaching colleagues in Social Work. Certainly Carl Rogers earlier work (1951) on client centered therapy would be useful. For Rogers, the message given back to the client by the interviewer is that of the client, nothing more, nothing less. The interviewer thus can escape the conspiracy that Matza correctly worries about. (Hey! We never said it would be easy!)

Also, and we're not entirely sure here, is the work of William Glaser and his reality therapy. (1964) This might work well. As we understand it, reality between client and practitioner is affected through the latter's--the practitioner's--constant control over the way the situation is defined. So, as earlier sociologists (Thomas, Cooley, Mead, Blumer especially; Loomis and Loomis 1965) would have the definition of the situation as a happening *outside* the direct control of individuals, the therapeutic situation would have a one-sided control by the therapist.

Along with the development of rapport, practitioners in Corrections need especially to be familiar with the language of the trade, the concepts of the social and behavioral sciences. We have recollection of a sixteen year old referred on a delinquent petition from a West suburban Chicago community. The boy was born to a middle class family, seven siblings, and he was severely retarded. The mother kept him home, caring for him, watching over and supervising him as best she could with such a large family. He was referred by the suburban Juvenile Police, and although the delinquent petition alleged delinquency as the general complaint, the actual court/police write-up "should have" been *beastiality*. Apparently, the officer only knew the street language, which was cause for both embarrassment and hilarity at the Court hearing.

The officer not only was unaware of extremely useful behavioral concepts, he was also unaware of correct referral policy. Fortunately, an understanding and experienced Judge put the case on track with an immediate dismissal and informal referral to the State Social Service Agency.

Now, in developing rapport we need to pay attention to meaning. David Riesman much earlier advised speaking directly to your audience. (1954) Practitioners in Corrections are aware that they must communicate directly with their clients. Although we empathize with practitioners in their dilemmas to communicate with clients, we do not believe that worthwhile relationships, long term and meaningful, are developed by "descending," so to speak, to the language of the street. Clients know when we are acting "outside of" our roles. We reject the advice by some well meaning practitioners to "use four letter words, over and over" in the communication interaction.

And yet, we must get our communication straight. Perhaps Clifford Shaw was right in insisting on his Street Workers having intimate knowledge of the community. Certainly the classical study on Street Corners by William Foote Whyte (1943) is a case in point. Whyte spent five years in the community before coming to grips with his study of the "gangs."

An example of really not knowing the communication frame of reference comes to mind. Back on October 23, 1983, our U.S. Marine Corps barracks in Beirut, Lebanon was bombed by the Shiite faction of the Moslems. To this day we still have a fuzzy picture of the ultimate responsibility where over two-hundred-fifty of our young Marines were killed and many others terribly wounded. A few days following the awful event President Reagan gave a television speech to the American people where he recounted the catastrophe, our resolve to stand fast, and he made a particularly emotional appeal by telling of a young Marine, hospitalized, severely wounded, paralyzed, unable to speak, who was yet able to trace out with his right hand and finger the words "*Semper Fi*" on a visiting Generals lapel. The General was commending and attempting to comfort all the wounded and hospitalized, while awarding the Purple Heart citation medal.

Someone on Reagan's staff should have told him of the double meaning of what the Marine traced out on the General's tunic! We all know, it is supposed, that the Marine Motto of *Semper Fidelis* is Latin that translates as Always Faithful. However, ..."*semper fi*" means something quite different. We won't print it here. Nicely stated, it connotes "bug off," "don't volunteer." These are the *nice* connotations. If you doubt, ask a Marine!

Now if the President with his staff could have made that kind of communication gaffe, how much language out of context, and foiled meanings are there in the relationship between Corrections Practitioners and clients? We have to assume that it is great. What needs to be done is to minimize the problem. President Reagan was able to escape any call for "damage control" on the part of his public relations people simply because there are not a lot of Marines -- former or present -- out there who knew what was being communicated.

Whenever we contemplate the field of Corrections we have to consider the large number who started careers and moved on to other places, other careers. The field has more than its share of drop-ins and drop-outs. As indicated previously in chapter one, a National Education Association official recently worried about opening primary-secondary teaching to those college grads that had not prepared by way of teacher education and state certification. "I am not interested in people who go into teaching for three or four years until they grow up and see what they want to do in life."(*Newsweek* 1990: 63, Keith Geiger). Those of us who have spent much time teaching and working in Corrections see an analogy that could easily be applied to our chosen work. And we are uncomfortable with it. Our instinct is to fight back. Our young people won't do this in Corrections. Won't they?

We must make the career ladder visible, open and understandable in Corrections. The teaching field has accomplished more than we have. Education's worry is about keeping what they have won. Corrections still has the battle ahead. And we think unionization is a key.

All fields of work, whether they are professions or *quasi*-so, as David Matza would say, have their own values, culture, language. The Police, according to Niederhoffer are perhaps more to themselves, clannish, and deliberately isolate themselves because they believe outsiders won't understand their peculiar type of involvement with the public -- both the criminal element and the honest public citizens.

Corrections, too, has its culture. We can point to Correction's "Black humor" for instance. Outsiders, and even novices to the Correctional field are often appalled at the kind of stories, euphemisms, anecdotes, cliches, and the like that are passed around. Newcomers have to be taken aside and explained that the "humor" is in reality only "letting off steam." Better to burn-up than burn-out! Black humor can be a way of handling the job. A veneer of hardness is developed around our precious presentation of self, lest we burn-out. This is one reason we would urge an abundance of empathy toward clients, ...and very little sympathy. More about this will be said later.

One such black humor joke had to do with a play on words taken out of psychoanalytic context. A way of making a recommendation for commitment to a correctional institution for a supposedly failed delinquent client was to advise the Judge that he "... had no lid on his *id!*" It used to bring about courtroom snickering, ... just before the commitment order.

One last set of actors in the field of Corrections need to be addressed. Wooden (1976) has urged that some of the people who want to go into Corrections go directly into the field of investigative reporting. He had done so personally, writing and "whistle blowing." Probably one of the most famous was Fred Wiseman for his documentary and film production of "Titicut Follies" (1967). This later was a depiction of the particularly de-humanizing experiences of mental hospital patients. It was so unflattering to the personnel at the Institution portrayed that Weisman was instantly awarded a kind of pariah status among institutional administrations. His work, though one is uneasy in reviewing it, remains brilliant.

For investigative reporting to take hold in Corrections, much more would have to occur. In the field of urban studies, Trownstine and Christensen (1982) have called for collaboration between the disciplines of journalism and social science. They make a case that strengths of the two bring about an in-depth analysis that could not be achieved otherwise. Their study of the power structure in Silicon Valley --San Jose, California-- reveals insights that the social scientist on his own would have missed; and also insights at understanding that the reporter on his own would have missed. Their work is a team effort, and little in social science literature has addressed this methodology. We expect much more will be made of this in coming years. What this means for the Correctional field can only be hoped; it will portend breakthroughs in our work with juveniles, and that will be for the good.

Finally, an old Juvenile Institution Chaplain once told us that the one virtue needed for actors in the field of Corrections was that of compassion.[8] We have never forgotten this. We know what he meant. And what he meant can't quite be written down.

We're reminded of the Reporter's story about the older woman being interviewed concerning her feelings about War and our young men being killed over there. The reporter told us that she had voiced her patriotism, and her hope that no one would die; that she was truly sorry about the situation, but that if push came to shove,...then it probably would get bloody. War was, after all, a hellish human experience. Then the reporter added, that it was only in the half-minute televised interview version that the "quivers" in her voice could really be seen and interpreted by the listeners. Compassion is like that quiver; it is that fleeting, heart-felt message of brotherly love.

ENDNOTES FOR CHAPTER TWO

1. Parole Chief Walter Wirtz of Illinois' Northern district (Cook, Lake and DuPage counties); Mr. Wirtz had most of his correctional experience prior to World War II. He brought intelligence, understanding, and compassion to his position. He was particularly and paternally influential with novices to the field.

2. February, 1990; visiting institutions where persons reside and live out their daily experiences can be most interesting. Individuals assigned the task of escort usually attempt to ascertain the experience background of visitors. Reciprocal knowledge and understandings immensely facilitates communication and dialogue. A lack of sophistication for the total living institution is quickly recognized by a guide or escort; when this is the case, visitors receive the "cook's tour": around and about as expediently as is appropriate.

Insider "savvy" and sophistication became particularly frustrated--and threatened--several years ago, in a conversation with an ex-convict who had had nearly thirty years confinement, mostly consecutive, in a State Prison. In response to the assertion that one of the authors made detailing his nine years live-in experience, the ex-con stated with authority: "...but *that* was from the other side of the bars!"

3. Juvenile institutions, particularly detention facilities, have resident populations with a wide array of social experience backgrounds. Some children and youth, referred to as the "institutionalized child," have been socialized to the total living arrangement. They usually fit-in rather quickly, adjusting and coping on their own terms. Staff at these institutions find that it is easier to run the daily activities when there are a few of these types present; all this does not bode well for the rest of the incarcerated population. We would venture to conclude that this is not good.

4. Much of the community studies research has focused on particular "typical" American communities. Most times communities were re-named for publication. Thus we have had Middletown (Morris, Illinois), Cerebrille (Blomington, Indiana), Yankee City (Muncie, Indiana), and others. More recently we have seen the publication of studies where the communities were directly identified, like San Jose and the whole of Silicon Valley by Trounstine and Christensen (1982).

This earlier penchant for anonymity in community studies appears to have run its course; this is probably just as well, as identity became common knowledge; there was just no way that anonymity could be maintained; it never was really effective in the first place. One would have to wonder *if* and *when* much of the anonymity and secrecy surrounding the correctional field will evolve in a similar way.

5. There has always been a sociological and popular interest in the parameters of work. Typically, Americans have been socialized through schooling to "love" their work; yet they are also asked "...do we work to live, or live to work?" Only relatively recently in the American lexicon has the word *workaholic* surfaced; it truly has the pejorative ring to it. Beginning workers in corrections have a particularly difficult time balancing the requirements of their position with personal needs.

The argument being developed here is that the *institution* of corrections has the *moral* and *expedient* obligation to look to the welfare of its staff.

6. Judge Charles Schudson of Milwaukee effectively began to administer the operation of the Juvenile Court from the judicial bench in the mid 1980's.

7. Coincidentally, the young lady recently contacted one of the authors of this monograph for a recommendation for the position of school guidance counselor in the local school system. Although not surprising, it is disquieting. We are witness to a skilled supervising practitioner with almost two decades experience looking to change careers. And it would be a change; the educational and correctional enterprises are not the same. Counseling delinquents is tough. Two positive considerations for her would be better economic compensation, and an easier work life; not more interesting, but definitely easier and financially more rewarding. But for all of this, we are saddened.

8. Father Raymond Grant, S.J. was chaplain at the Arthur J. Audy Home for Children (Chicago/Cook County's juvenile detention facility) for many years. His life of service to God and community was an inspiration not only to the many delinquents he consoled and counseled, but also to many of the practitioners in corrections.

3
The Protagonist

The central character in delinquency drama has been the deviant figure, the *jeune premiere*. All of us are drawn to consider him, whether we view his presence with revulsion and disdain or sympathy and benevolent concern. Roget (1977) would draw our attention to the protagonist's role as a "heavy," not particularly attaching our admiration because of heroic or admirable qualities; acting out his lines and performance more in line with what Tannenbaum (1938) has described as the "dramatization of evil."[1]

We are aware that addressing delinquency as a social problem phenomena requires that the distinction be made between the role performance of an individual delinquent on the one hand, and widespread delinquent acts on the other. Most considerations of this subject differentiate between these two: the Act and the Actor! And yet, even though the distinction is made, further considerations between the two are often so blurred that we must wonder about the implications for public policy that flow from current research and analysis of this problem. For instance, different kinds of control should be implemented if we want to discourage widespread delinquent acts, rather than rehabilitate a particular delinquent or even a type of delinquent. In controlling for shoplifting acts, many store managers have come to rely upon the modern technology of video surveillance, one-way mirrors, move-spanning cameras, the fish-eye mirrors, and so forth. But in attempting to stop or reform particular shoplifters or types, different strategies are called for.

We once knew of a juvenile "gang" (actually a group of about six very young juveniles) that shoplifted from department stores, but they had added a new dimension to their deviant activity. They shoplifted from one store, ...

43

but added the goods to a second store's inventory; from the second store they shoplifted adding this to a third store. Thus their delinquent caper, laughable as it was, became a kind of subtraction and addition of inventories. While the modern technologies were responsible for their subsequent capture, eventual reform could only occur through human interaction. Someone had to talk to them and with them.

We don't want to spend too much time on the distinction between the act and the actor in delinquency. It is so overly obvious. Let it suffice to say that by further drawing attention to the two different social phenomena, we hope to clear some of the confusion that is in the study, not only of delinquency, but of all of deviance considerations.

There are many delinquency textbooks and quite a number of monograph studies on particular topics. In the earlier part of this century and up until recently, gang and gang activities of juveniles occupied a central concern. A reasonable assessment will show that two topics are always -- or most always -- addressed: definition and magnitude. What *is* the social problem of delinquency AND to what extent does it exist?

Concerning definition: For a very long time the social sciences -- particularly sociology -- framed a definition of delinquency as a *role* performance. Deviation from accepted and/or acceptable practices became the benchmark of measurement and analysis. It was always somewhat uncomfortable to entertain thoughts as to whose norms were being applied in setting standards. But the social scientist proceeded to "pick apart" the definition of delinquency, sometimes calling it behavior which, if identified, would result in fulfilling definitional requirements; sometimes calling it a *resistance potential*, (Robison 1960:199) defined by what others were willing to do about behavior of delinquents.

This latter interpretation would remind the sociologist of that particular type of norm that is called a *sanction*. Focus on action is upon the negative, the punishment aspect of the behavioral equation.

Some authors even refused to come directly to grips with a definition, preferring to use such terms as misconduct, (Arnold and Brungardt 1983); or simply bad boys.[2] And while we always knew that early century legal definitions encompassed behavior that was at one extreme felonious acts and the other extreme the status offenses, it was not until recently that delinquency texts began to directly refer to the adolescent criminal (Flowers, 1990).

Early on in this century crime and criminal behavior was excluded from the review of the Juvenile Court; social scientists of all persuasions -- sociology, social work, education, even the legal profession -- had eschewed the notion that delinquency was in any way criminal behavior. That was in the past. In the 1990's we wonder about the concept of delinquency. Will it be completely subsumed under a definition of crime? While we think that this will not be the case, enough confusion and anxiety exists in the field of corrections over a reasonably workable definition for delinquency to urge thoughtful dialogue among the experts. The older legal definition of delinquency held for the better part of this century; and although we knew of its limitations and flaws, the very least that can be said of it was that it tended to unify a field of study that was separate from other social problem concerns. Delinquency was at once separated and distinguishable as a special social science interest.

Concerning the prevalence of delinquency, two preoccupations among the experts appear. One is the speculation as to its extent as a social problem today. Usually the question asked was "how much delinquency is there?" Or, "are the kids all bad?" The reference point, usually unstated, is to some by-gone past. The image of a contented America portrayed in the earlier issues of the *Saturday Evening Post*'s drawings by Norman Rockwell comes to mind.

The other preoccupation is the speculation as to how much delinquency exists that is hidden. How much deviance of all sorts goes on that we just don't know about? There is the kind of populist portrayal of things getting worse; that delinquency, crime and all sorts of deviance are not only rising and getting out of hand, but that much of what we do know about remains hidden from public scrutiny. There is also a popular perception that these types of social problems -- especially delinquency and crime -- have a very large base of undetected, none-the-less committed offenses. How accurate is all of this perception, *albeit* speculation?

In addressing the above thoughts and concerns we would first call attention to MacIver's (1967:3-26) conclusion with respect to increasing delinquency. The best word to describe this would be "impressionistic." In the early part of this century this used to be the "code word", meaning what was believed to be true, but which lacked empirical verification; and also that such objectivity as would be satisfied with and through empirical verification was not possible. Such is the case with the impression of increasing delinquency, at all levels -- rates, hidden juvenile delinquency assessments, and percents at risk assessments. (Percents at risk only include those who could be in the category. For instance infants and the elderly are obviously excluded in any classification scheme of juvenile delinquency.)

Experts have argued for years about whether or not delinquency or crime was increasing. Although we know of many who argue that there is an increase in the problem and numbers for delinquency, we know equally well of those who argue that there is *no* increase. Any apparent increase, these latter argue, stems from more sophisticated techniques of data gathering, more officials working in the field, and so forth. In short, they argue that the "net has been made larger."

No experts we are aware of argue that delinquency or crime has actually diminished. So if the experts are divided into three groups--one arguing increase, another arguing no change, and a third that is either without opinion or has no advocates--then it is reasonable to assert that there is an impression of increase in delinquency in the last few generations.

On *Hidden Delinquency:* There are really two notions to the idea of a hidden group of delinquents. One concerns those that remain undetected; those who never were apprehended. Most of the questionnaires looking to hidden delinquency assessment employ anonymity for the respondent in the hope of tapping an otherwise unavailable source of data and information.

Then there are those delinquents who remain hidden because of some form of favoritism. The popular press and the public myth are much concerned with the youth who is caught, but because of family and social class background, is released. There is just enough truth involved to make the belief credible. America has always been uncomfortable with the idea that an upper crust of society (the upper classes) is able to get away with mischief. Much of the popular literature is aimed at showing how justice prevails in the end, and that even the wealthiest of individuals and families must pay for transgressions. But there is also an opposite message, and not only from the radical left writers, that the upper classes are insulated from paying for their crime and their children's delinquency.

Also quite popular among fictional writers and also a significantly large segment of those that consider themselves professionals in corrections, is that theme that we are *all* guilty, that "...but for the 'Grace of God,'" we would all have been caught and appropriately punished for our hidden transgressions. Most of the scientific attempts to tap into the extent of hidden delinquency, from Porterfield's (1946) earlier research, to a number of more recent scholars, all show that delinquency, crime and deviance of all sorts (special attention is sometimes given to sexual aberrations) are widespread. Some of the inquiries into this are clever, attempting to differentiate on the basis of seriousness of delinquency, frequency of delinquency and so forth. But the latest thinking on the subject remains, delinquency is widespread and ...

largely undetected.

Yet the questions still remain. We seem uncomfortable with our research findings and our impressions. This is especially true because we know also from respectable studies that those who are caught and punished are most represented by the lower classes, the urban poor, and the minority populations.

We would urge caution in accepting, too easily, the conclusion stated above that delinquency is omnipresent. We make this *caveat* for three reasons:

1. A problem of comparability. If we accept delinquency as widespread, then the classical experiment is suspect; no control group is possible. The definition of delinquency itself is nullified.

2. A practical problem. If we accept delinquency as widespread, then our democratic institutions and ideals become jaundiced. There is the implication of a fickle community enforcement of norms. The impact on trust is immeasurable. Trust is at the base of all community cohesion.

3. A problem of misallocation of funds. In the past several decades most of the funding for delinquency prevention programs has been targeted for the inner city, where the urban and ethnic poor are located. It so happens that this *is* where most delinquency occurs, given our official definitions. Those that are caught and adjudicated are considered to be delinquent. But *if* delinquency *is* widespread, cutting across class lines,...?

Concerning this last point on funding, we would not urge reallocation to the upper class communities. Our point is that there is a kind of social/political argument going on. We once had occasion to argue with a criminal justice colleague who firmly believed that delinquency was widespread, and that the upper classes, the WASP's, were involved in as much,even more, delinquency than were the inner city, poor ethnics. After long argument, calling attention to a kind of *normative dispersion* of delinquency, where delinquency patterns could be observed to occur, more likely in the inner city, our argument came to a standoff. Neither would give an inch. We asked them,... "why not spend our time, our talent, and our treasure focusing on *his* source of the problem, the affluent suburb?" His answer was silence. A political agenda had been identified.

While we are uncomfortable in our arguments above, we would note that money is a claim on social activity. In the past history of corrections, dollars spent have very often had a corrupting effect. More often than not, problem solving in delinquency has taken second place to social and political messages. We do argue that more dialogue and "research" must be given to the vexing problem of hidden delinquency.

Years back we noticed that the upper classes, with their intact family structures, often provided alternatives in punishment for the transgressions of their children. Such would be the case when it became overly obvious that "something" was going to happen to their offspring as a result of court action. Instead of commitment to State Training schools, upper class parents often came up with the alternative of a placement in private military academies. Even placement at Gibault School for boys in Indiana (a former home of Charles Manson) attracted the placement of some boys who otherwise would have ended up in state facilities. Was this favoritism? It can be argued both ways. Certainly some boys "got off" as compared to others whose families lacked initiative, concern, ...and even money. A strong case could be made, however, that these military academies were "harder" on the boys than the State correctional institutions. That they in *no* way lacked discipline, we believe, is indisputable.

A final note on hidden delinquency. We do not believe it is randomly scattered, no matter how ubiquitous it appears. Perhaps it is better to view the delinquency problem as normatively dispersed, or culturally diffused. It is there, and it is large and it appears to be growing. But then again so it is with many social phenomena, like the tendency for more education or the tendency for greater mobility. We need to know the social conditions that make these more possible.

As we proceed to consider delinquency it would appear preferable not to view it as a social role. There are times when society may want to try to moderate the social problem by simply considering delinquent acts. As indicated previously, all sorts of activities could be enjoined to diminish delinquency: more and better lighting, curfew, teaching courses like marriage and family readiness in secondary schools. There are correlates to the problem. But these would not add to our understandings.

We started this monograph noting that cities call for distinct ways of living. There are patterns of urban conduct that are called for in getting along with each other. That coping with city living also may be self fulfilling is probably secondary to the ongoing processes of urbanism and urbanization. They are reciprocal as processes, and yet humans must come to terms with their impact. As social and human processes, after all, they are not truly natural; except, of course, in the sense that human activity is natural. This is the argument that all of cultural content is in itself natural.

Much attention in delinquency has been given to role modeling. The way it has been presented is that "if only" young persons are exposed to correct "role models," things would work out. It is submitted that the social role as a theoretical social system is only *one* of *four*, according to one of our more profound sociological theorists, the late Florian Witold Znaniecki. In one of his more significant treatises (*Cultural Sciences*, 1952), he posits that there is an evolutionary process working in human nature that produces, from simple to complex, four social systems: (1) social relations, (2) social roles, (3) social groups, and (4) national cultural origins (ethnics). (Mackey, Miller, and Fredericks 1989).

Why social roles has been the focus of attention for so long is a bit of a mystery. That the social role has had the unique quality of being quite fragile has been observed by others. (Banton 1965). It is a little like the Christmas tree ornament: glittery, shinning, fascinating on the outside, ...but... don't handle it too tightly. That we play many roles in life is obvious to both poets and social scientists. The search for a "key role" is probably illusory. Such concepts as key roles are useful in particular research ventures and in teaching freshmen introductory courses in sociology. But are they elsewhere?

Before we mentioned a concept that we introduced and we called it the "actor-role congruency fallacy." Though it is close to the confusion that takes place when collective representations are substituted for the individual or *vice versa* (the aggregative fallacy), it is different in that it refers to an individual and the roles he plays, or might play. Thus, which young person would characterize himself by a particular role? What individual would describe himself as always one type of social person or another? As we noted in Chapter Two, a guard at an institution is not always the "bully." Similarly, what young person would subscribe to the particular role of "fighter?" This sounds a lot like labeling theory all over again, but we submit that people do interact, and they do this in prearranged, normative ways.

It seems it would be preferable to focus on that social system of interpersonal relations that might be called, as above, social relations. Erving Goffman (1959) spent much of his time describing the sets of social relations, those little measures of behavior, patterned as they are, that help us get along. The trouble with this is that most role types would be of limited use. But that these social relations would serve us in a better understanding in our modern, urban society seems probable. A distinct advantage to concentrating on social relations as a concept for delinquency, is that we would recognize their clear transition effect. Social relations quite clearly evolve over time; they become more stable in society, taking on more depth, and eventually, they become roles in themselves. This is the way the theory is interpreted. We would also be able to try to educate, to socialize getting along together. It would be easier to socialize for particular interactions, like being courteous in everyday life. Social relations are at a lower level of ordered relations than are social roles.

We have in mind a few "case histories,"... stories about delinquents from the past. The individuals referred to were involved in particular and peculiar relationships that brought them to the attention of the authorities. For the most part court workers, from judge to social worker, on through institution attendants (guards) would try to infer some key role -- delinquent -- from particular fractured ways of behaving. From the first sentence of this paragraph the astute reader will note that we find it difficult also *not* to categorize. But we do want to pay attention to the debilitating and fractured social relations described as deviant.

The *Stigmatic*: A boy was referred to Chicago's Juvenile Court in the mid-1950's for auto larceny. He was involved with several others, all juveniles. After an initial and official Court Hearing, his case would have been placed on 'special supervision' (a kind of official probation) for about nine months. After such time, it would have been dismissed if no further violations were evident. Such was the court's policy at the time. Given the kind of rehabilitative model of diagnosing behavior that was current then, it was obvious he "needed help." The boy was sixteen, black, and from the inner city, ethnic enclave; his family was urban poor. Additionally, however, he had the kind of stigmata that causes social workers to pay close attention. He had no nose. In infancy his nose had been destroyed, "eaten off,"by rodents -- rats -- while he lay in his crib. To the other boys in his "gang,"(not really a gang, but a collection of juveniles, organized around 'joy riding'") he had the nick-name of "dog-face." His facial features were most ugly; his nostrils, or what there was of his face, constantly "oozed," so the membranes appeared pink and fragile. Looking at him one could only be reminded of Goffman's work, (1963) where the onlooker constantly gazes elsewhere, anywhere but at the stigmatized, avoiding eye contact. This was the kind of social interaction with others that was the everyday life of this boy. He appeared mostly withdrawn, quiet, and the butt of much of the conversations among his juvenile peers.

There was a kind of happy ending to this story though. His case was assigned to one of the few probation officers who saw to it that he received corrective surgery. Unfortunately, many of the court workers, then as now, would have been more concerned with the reason for referral, the official police charge, than with the extenuated and obvious problems. A little over a year later his face looked "pretty good." The plastic surgeons had done wonders. The young adolescent's nose looked almost as good as if God and nature had been the giver. This kind of a case goes a long way in arguing for the rehabilitative model. We're not sure what kind of "help" he would have received without becoming involved in an auto larceny referral. Much argument, of course, can be made that the wrong social agency -- the Juvenile Court -- became the prime care-giver in getting plastic surgery. But it should also be observed,... where were the teachers, the guidance counselors, the principals, the school people, the parents or guardians? He had, after all been involved in the Chicago Public School System. Where, also were any of the community people, ministers, aldermen, and others? Was there no good Samaritan neighbor in the community?

Incidentally, one thing that Mayor Richard Daley, the first Mayor Richard Daley, should be remembered for is his introduction of Rodent Control in Chicago.[3] It was extremely common for children to be rat-bitten before the late 1950's, although problems such as described were far less frequent. Most of us are aware of the problem of lead poisoning that was most common in the inner cities; very young children "chewed" window sills, furniture, almost anything that *all* youngsters are wont to do. The problem of lead poisoning arose because lead based paints had been used. Still another problem that arose in city living was that of very young children eating candied aspirin (solicitating intoxication). As many as *eight* such cases per day came to the attention of County medical people. And this would only account for those that had not sought private medical service!

The *Tragedian*: Quite another story, one with not-so-happy an ending involved Gerald, a sixteen year old from Oak Park, Illinois. He was referred to Juvenile Court, alleged a delinquent, for stealing an auto. His family background included one younger brother and single parent, the mother. She was raising the two boys as best she could; actually she had a reasonably well-paid job as a legal secretary. The three could best be described as "middle class." The mother was devoted to her boys. Psychiatrists would later call the relationship overly possessive, in the true Freudian sense. Her husband had deserted her and the boys to fend for themselves while they were still infants. He was not in the social picture.

As was Court policy at the time, Gerald was placed on Special Supervision -- again a "kind" of official probation. He quickly became involved, within several weeks, in two to three further auto larcenies. The third time he again appeared in court on a new petition alleging delinquency. He had stolen an auto and was "joy riding" the vehicle -- he was the driver --

around Oak Park on an early summer evening, along with some rider-only friends.

An off-duty police-man noticed the car and its occupants. Gerald was slight of stature, looked younger than his sixteen years, and probably did not appear the most proficient motor vehicle operator. The policeman physically grabbed the slower moving vehicle, linking his arm through the opened front and rear side door windows. At that point Gerald sped up the vehicle. The policeman had a short, fast ride, holding on to the outside of the car. Fortunately, when he was thrown from the speeding vehicle, he landed in a patch of weeds with not much more damage than his dignity.

When the case came to the Court's attention the mother was advised that as Court policy stood, Gerald would be committed to the State Training School. She was most distraught. On the social worker's advice, she was told of the possibility of private, alternative placement. She became a "prime-mover," affecting the acceptance of Gerald at the Gibault School for Boys located just outside of Terre Haute, Indiana. In as much as that school's general policy was to accept no more than two Illinois boys each year, she did provide Yeoman's effort at having them accept her son. It is doubtful that without her persistence her son would have been accepted.

At the actual court hearing, all was ready for the Judge to allow Gerald to be placed at Gibault in lieu of incarceration at the State Training School.

But when time came to adjudicate the case, the policewoman, a juvenile officer from Oak Park objected to the placement, and in open court addressed the charges most damagingly for Gerald. She spoke about the "evil of the deed," the "hardness of Gerald's heart," and the almost fatality of the off-duty policeman. In telling this story, we do not want to convey an underestimation of event. It could have been quite, quite serious. The Court's Probation Staff at that time always viewed alternative plans to the State Training School placement as superior. Not-with-standing, the Judge was most influenced by the juvenile officer's indictment. (As a point of information, Judges were most reluctant to appear lenient when very pointed and damaging testimony went into the Court Reporter's record. This is the political reality of our Justice System; perhaps they realize all too well the poor publicity outcomes if their lenience later appears ill-placed.) For Gerald, the Judge ordered commitment to the State Facility.

A few hours after the hearing the Judge was approached. He indicated that he felt no other court order was feasible after such uncompromising testimony was entered into the court record. However, he indicated that Gerald should be held in the court's adjacent detention home for about a week, after which time he would vacate the commitment order. This followed and Gerald was placed privately at Gibault.

About a year and one-half later, Gerald was back on the streets of Oak Park, having been released from Gibault. He was being supervised by a Catholic Social Services (Chicago) Worker, as was the arrangement between Gibault and this agency.

Gerald was killed while either in the process of stealing a hub-cap from an expensive car, -- or perhaps tying his shoe. No one ever really knew which. On a west-side Chicago avenue, near Oak Park, the owner of the vehicle that Gerald was kneeling next to, came out on his front porch and shot Gerald, killing him instantly. The shot severed Gerald's carotid artery.

As kind of an epilogue to this story, the man who fired the pistol was indicted by a Grand Jury for manslaughter; however, his case was acquitted at trial. And as a final note to the tragedy, about a year later the man committed suicide.

In telling these true stories there ought be a point made, besides the obvious moral, legal, and civic implications. For our monograph it is that Gerald occupied no social role that would fit under the rubric of delinquent. He did have inappropriate social relations -- with his mother, his social worker, the police, and many others. He really did not cope well. At the time, the Court Psychiatrist made much of the relationship with his mother; but that was standard practice in those days, to invoke large dosages of psychiatric and psychoanalytic theory. We would prefer to keep it simple, concentrating on those social relations that appeared obvious. That he had no adult male role model was evident; but we think this is insufficient to really understand the tragedy. If only he could have found excitement and fulfillment in the simple social relations that most youngsters do -- like doing well in a particular sport, or academic, or extra-curricular school activity. The list of such simple, yet less than role involvement activities would seem endless.

Murder in the Second Degree: Quite another story involved a sixteen year old boy from the near West side of Chicago. He was black, and probably a member of the Egyptian Cobra gang whose "territory" had the unusual name of "K-town." This was because most of the streets running north-south in this area of the west side of Chicago had names beginning with the letter K: Kedzie, Karlov, Kistner, Kostner, etc. This area was the "turf" of street gangs like the Vice Lords, Egyptian Cobras and others. He was of a single parent home; his mother, and the family would best be described as urban, poorer, lower class...not impoverished, but poor. His first name was Chance; we're not sure of the reason or origin of his name.

(An incidental footnote to names: one of the resident physicians from the County hospital told us one time of his various encounters with young, indigent, obstetric patients. Apparently some of the young girls, euphoric after delivery, emotionally attached to their deliverer--the resident physician--sought advice on naming their child. The advice: such names as "Placenta," and "Umbilical." We would laugh except for the crying.)

Chance came to the attention of the Juvenile Court in as much as a rather violent purse-snatch-killing had occurred in his community. An elderly woman, a private school librarian in her late fifties was on her way home on a late autumn afternoon when her purse was snatched. Some not-too-reliable witnesses had seen a young man run from behind, grab her shoulder purse, and when she didn't -- or couldn't -- release it fast enough, the young man jabbed her in the back with an ice pick. The woman apparently in shock, staggered to her apartment which was nearby; she had lived all her life in the neighborhood, over fifty years; but it had changed from a close-knit community of families, with single ethnic background, homogenous religious backgrounds, etc., to one of inner city breakdown. There were a few apartments in which older tenants resided. Mostly these were area residents who had not moved from the area and neighborhood, and she was one of them.

A neighbor would best be described as a person who lived in proximity for this inner city area. A neighbor observed the woman in a state of shock, fumbling to enter her apartment. She was able to take her to a near-by doctor's office along Roosevelt Road. The physician refused first aid, apparently because she had no identification (her purse had been snatched). There was no way he would be remunerated. The neighbor took the woman back to her apartment, where they were able to gain access. The woman died shortly thereafter. The coroner's autopsy revealed that the tip of the ice-pick had broken off and had become lodged in her spine.

Several things followed. The newspapers raked the physician "over the coals," probably justifiably, for his insensitivity in not giving emergency care to the woman. After a while, the professional Medical Associations also checked in for an investigation of malpractice. Interestingly, we have observed all sorts of work associations when one of their members is accused of wrongdoing: judges; patrolmen; even, as we noted above, Doctors of

Medicine. The first inclination is unchallenged support for the member, incensed support, seemingly in the face of overwhelming evidence to the contrary. Finally, the Associations "throw the rascal out."

But more of interest to us was that the area police Juvenile Officer told a group of correctional workers -- judges, probation officers, prosecutors, detention staff -- that he would "go find the boy." He did! Within a day! Later on we asked the Juvenile Officer "how he did it?" His reply was that the communication network was "solid." The juveniles in the area know and tell. He was an exceptionally astute police juvenile officer who knew his area.

The same day Chance was referred to detention he was interviewed by two homicide detectives. They apparently felt the case was not tight. Anyway Chance had to be awakened about eleven P.M. The officers interrogated him on the authorization of the presiding Juvenile Court Judge. Even then, which preceded the Miranda warning and the juvenile Gault cases, the juvenile justice system was concerned with constitutional privileges, but not in the same way as today. Chance would not be interviewed today without a lawyer present.

The two officers did get a confession [4] from Chance. Actually they played the "good cop, bad cop" game on him. This was sometimes called the "Mutt and Jeff" routine. For those readers interested in the social psychological theoretical underpinning to this inter-relational strategy, see Bruno Bettleheim's vivid description and analysis of German *schutte staffel* (SS) treatment of Jewish prisoners at Auschwitz. (Macoby, Newcombe, and Hartley 1952).

Chance's reason for referral on a delinquency petition was serious enough that on a *venue* motion from the prosecutor, he was waived to criminal court. Several months later, at the trial hearing on a manslaughter charge, the Juvenile Court's detention record was subpoenaed. It seems that the trial prosecutors had erred, saying that Chance confessed -- but in a different place, a police district. The defense attorney who was quite astute and interested in Chance, noted the error and sought to challenge the confession's authenticity: it was not possible for Chance to confess if he was in a location other than where the confession took place.

Anyway, Chance was convicted and sentenced to the State Prison System for a seven year term. He was paroled in a little over four years. Subsequently we had heard he was killed in a gang related shoot-out.

The *Arsonist*: There is the old Probation Officer's *caveat* about case histories. Watch out how you handle cases that involve "fire or kinky sex." We knew of only one boy ever referred for necrophilia (look it up if you don't understand), but we've seen several referred for playing with fire. Whether it's labeled arson or pyromania depends on those with whom you are talking.

Anyway, we remember this one boy, referred for setting fire to a large apartment complex on Chicago's near North side. He was white, sixteen, lower class, single parented, not much of a home life. Several persons lost their lives in the blaze. The journalists had a touching story for a few days, until it was concluded that all had been accidental. A tragic accident, but none-the-less, an accident.

The boy's referral to the Juvenile Court triggered a social history write-up that revealed a child with desperately poor home conditions. Arson charges always trigger psychiatric evaluation. Here he was evaluated, no special personality problems, but he did possess a strikingly high I.Q. score. At that time, the Director of Arden Shore, a private, handsomely endowed, institution along Lake Michigan's North shore, had instituted the policy of accepting only very, very bright youngsters. Boys that were accepted to Arden Shore could look forward to an almost unlimited educational opportunity. The institutions low client to staff ratio, together with its low population and classy surroundings made it "the" ideal place, a place that proponents of the rehabilitation model could only dream. He was accepted, and we can only hope and guess, lived happily ever after.

Not to be factitious, the story seemed to have a happy ending. The Director at Arden Shore would take a lot of criticism from agency social workers that she was overly elitist; but Josephine Strode ran a tight ship and she should be remembered. As a young girl she had her indoctrination into the welfare system at the University of Chicago, rubbing elbows with the likes of Jane Addams, Julia Lathrop, John Dewey, and others.

Another facet to this story was most intriguing. When it was concluded that the fire was "accidental," the newspaper's constant focus on the tragedy, which went on for several weeks, caused prosecutors to take some action. A "slum-lord" was found; old ordinances about owning unsafe properties were dusted off; a full-time public high school teacher and part-time "slum lord" was brought in and questioned by the police. For whatever reason, he was finger printed and his prints revealed that he was wanted on a fugitive warrant from twenty years earlier. He had apparently fled Detroit rather than go to court on a homicide charge, came to Chicago and passed himself off as having the educational credentials to teach English. He had done so for two decades until this apparent "fluke" caught up with him. We had known him from a few years earlier as he was married to one of his slum tenants. He had moved her and her five children to Oak Park and an upper middle class residential life style. One of the woman's young sons was brought to the Court's attention on an auto larceny. Interviews with him as step-father did not provide an inkling of his double life or an assumed status.

The Rapist: Robert was sixteen, white and middle class. His mother had remarried and the family of three were living together without seeming mishap. Both parents worked and apparently spent all that they earned. The social history would report -- rather puritanically for the 1990's, but not so for the '50's'-- that they "over spent." In the present generation we would refer to this couple with the acronym DINC -- Double Income; No Children; except, of course, there was Robert.

The parents were away vacationing in Florida. It was the school year, and Robert was left at home. On a Saturday night he journeyed to some of the risque (at that time) peep shows in downtown Chicago. Later this was invoked as partial defense; that he was somehow excited thru the exotic dancing that he had witnessed. On his way home he hid behind a railroad trestle long enough to surprise a woman, in her forties, where he raped her and beat her. The circumstances of his capture are forgotten, but he did confess to police.

Later he was to ask of his social worker-probation officer about the circumstances of his confession. He suspected that he had been "duped" into confessing, because he doubted the police had the kind of evidence they claimed to have. They didn't of course. But equally, and of course, Robert did commit rape, as he re-confessed to the Probation Officer. His interest was not in civil liberties, which it would be today, but in his suspicion of having been duped.

Robert was sixteen, as stated above. He did appear in Juvenile Court as no waiver was motioned by the prosecutor. Meanwhile, the mother returned home, most distraught at her son's predicament. She hired a private, well paid, "good" attorney, but an attorney that was completely unfamiliar with the Juvenile Court. The attorney saw all the files, interviewed Robert, and concluded that it would be in Robert's best interest to go along with a recommendation for commitment to the State Training School.

The average length of stay for a sixteen year old would be about seven to nine months; perhaps a few more as this was a rather serious case.

The mother intervened, insisting that her attorney plead Robert' innocence. Actually there are no pleas in Juvenile Court. The adjudicatory process is different from that found in adult criminal courts. The probation staff would come to conclude that the mother's solicitude was interference. Robert was not then provided with a Public Defender as he would be today. The best he had going for him was the probation staff in a kind of child advocacy role.

The mother insisted that the woman must have been a part of the crime; that the woman must, somehow, have enticed Robert. The victim did not; the victim never saw Robert until he hit her. But the mother insisted and persisted. Her attorney did as she asked. She had hired him. The Juvenile Judge postponed the hearing in order to bring in all of the pertinent evidence. In this time period, when confessions involving juveniles were part of the evidence, the police officers that were part of the confession process very often did not appear at an original juvenile court hearing. This is the kind of case that would argue well for *child advocacy*; that the lawyer representing a child *is* the child's representative, and no one else, not even the parent. We say this here even knowing that Robert did indeed rape this young grandmother.

During the period of case continuance Robert was held in detention. During this few week period he turned seventeen, an adult by statutory definition.

He was indicted by a Grand Jury, brought to trial in Criminal Court, convicted, and sentenced to seventy-five years in the State Penitentiary. At the time, the minimum he would end up serving would be one-third of the sentence -- twenty-five years. This is if everything went well for him during incarceration. We don't know whatever happened to Robert; except that he did go to prison.

The Poisoner:[5] One final case history involved the pathetic story of a twelve year old white boy, from an upper class background. George's parents were both professional; the father was a lawyer, and the mother a school teacher. There were a few siblings in the family, one pre-school. George was born with Down's Syndrome, plus he had the extreme debilitation of *spinal bifida*.

At twelve, when he was referred to Court, he had been attending special school for the severely handicapped. Each morning he was picked up by a school bus from his home. Later psychiatric examination and psychological work-up placed his I.Q. at about eighty to eighty-five. Additionally, the court psychiatrist pegged him as a sociopath.

George's reason for referral came from his family. He had been putting borax into the cereal food of his pre-school sibling and the grandmother, who were still in the house after the others had departed for the day, and before he was picked up by his school bus. Apparently he had been putting borax in their food for several days before he was found out. It caused sickness, dehydration and vomiting, but was not lethal.

During George's detention, which was for several months, his parents, or others, did not visit. Superficially, and at a first encounter with George, one would conclude that he was brighter than he actually tested out. His social class background had rubbed off on him somewhat. He even asked to have books on the classics; he was given reading material, but clinically he did as poorly as his tests revealed. He was "starved for attention," always wanting to talk to social workers about Plato, or Socrates, or...?

The Court worker recommended foster home placement; the psychiatrist suggested this would be dangerous. After several months he was placed back in his home. Over the weekend he had managed -- walking was extremely difficult -- to go to the kitchen of the home, turn on all the gas jets, and had attempted to do away with the entire sleeping family. He was returned to detention.

After a few more months detention, the Court worker was at a loss regarding George's placement disposition. Up until this point he had not been filed upon in a formal delinquent petition. He was, after all, only twelve years old, with pathetically severe handicaps.

We were present one time when an administrator asked George why he had chosen borax to put in his grandmother and little sister's food. After knowing George for awhile you would recognize that he was deadly serious about what he had done. Perhaps it was his low IQ that gave him a sort of *naivete*. His answer "...it was the only thing I could find." Given the extremely lethal and deadly products around most American homes, we would have to conclude that, at least, a tragedy of major proportions had not come to be. After all, he had not found the Drano under the sink.

George was unusual in detention though. Oddly enough, he was not "picked upon" by the other pre and post adjudicated delinquents. Because of his physical limitations, he was somewhat separated from the normal detention routine, but it would have been impossible to block off all contact with other detained juveniles. Our inference was that George made a presentation of self that others avoided, particularly his age peers. He was, frankly, a little "scary."

George was eventually committed to the State Training School following a court hearing on a delinquency petition. No one really wanted this kind of a disposition; the State Training School officials objected on the basis of his physical disabilities, noting that their Cottage System would be difficult to maneuver for George. This was true. They even objected, writing that George would be a target for the street wise, tough delinquent population of the State facility. This would NOT be true. Not once George was able to locate their kitchen!

Remarks on Six cases of Delinquency:

The six cases of juveniles involved in deviant actions that resulted in Juvenile Court adjudication may be interesting in their own light. Certainly we can gain some insights into the tangled web of human interaction. But there must be better reasons for including them here, in a discussion of what we have called the protagonist. If anything, it is to show the large diversity of human actions that account for juvenile justice interest. No one would want to argue that these cases are typical of those that come to the attention of the authority structure of society. But then again,...is it possible to argue that there is a typical auto larcenist, a typical runaway, a typical shoplifter, ...?

What we would want to point out are the fractured social relations, not necessarily best defined as role performances, that represent ways of life that end up as inferior ways of coping for the individual. These social relations are fragmentary, for the most part transitory parts of a whole life.

It would not be possible to explain these several cases with any common thread. Indeed, explanations of any one of these, centered around descriptive evidence of family discord, particularly as it related to the mothers "role." Psychoanalytic theory was often meshed with family explanations of causation -- aetiology -- by reference to "a lack of mothering," or "no adult male role models," or "oedipal complexes," or "absentee parenting." But in the end, are we left with any more ease that we have come to reliable and valid understandings? We think not.

Perhaps the better way to understand would be to concentrate on those social relations that are at the source of a problem. We will not always know what these may be for an individual. It might be best in individual cases to go on to other forms of social relations, other ways of life that allow better coping. What is being suggested here is to look forward, to the future, for particular individuals. It seems that too often a particular emphasis on the past only inhibits obtaining our goals. It is understandable in delinquency that the past experiences, conduct, behavior, reasons for referral, and so forth play a part in any review, judicial or otherwise. The implication we see in all of this is to not let the past determine the outcome, our goals of better ways of life for individuals.

And if we are of the mind that the past for us as an individual is that, *in the past*, the very least we can gain from continued study of the social problems of delinquency are further insights on how to help others. Prevention in the Criminal Juvenile Justice System has always taken a back seat to Control, an after the fact remedy. Knowing those social relations that are bound to be troublesome for juveniles to cope with will aid us in helping them cope. Too little attention is given in education and all of the socializing experiences for young persons today. We read about the "apprentice system" of a by-gone era and wonder how best we could implement pedagogy today. In our efforts to democratize education, to institutionalize and formalize the processes of socialization, we have lost much of the interpersonal relations that are at the heart of coping with everyday life problems. This is more exacerbated in modern urban, industrialized, bureaucratized society. (Stein 1960).

But whereas our understandings seem to grow with regard to how society and the system works, we seem "hell bent" on using that same system to cure the problems. Or, opposing this, calling on doing away with the system altogether in large, significant ways. We do not ever envision private or even volunteer sources as an answer to educating our youth; this is perhaps the middle ground to a solution of social problems. It neither advocates complete dispersal of the system nor encouragement of system growth. We think the system must be kept intact, particularly the educational and juvenile justice systems. There are social roles to be played: teachers, counselors, probation officers, judges. These are whole roles, careers, as in contradistinction to the social relations that juveniles play out. Our interest here is in pointing out social relations that don't work for young people. If we believe in social theory, that social relations are incipient role formations, that social relations have not yet taken on the permanence of what the sociologist believes of the role system, then we might concentrate our efforts at helping to socialize young people to get along in society. Too much attention in the schools has been placed on job placement. While this is a necessary part of any curriculum, it is not enough! The schools and the teachers need to do more. But more can only be accomplished with societal approbation.

On Confidentiality in the Juvenile Justice System:

Of all the values that surround the relationship of the juvenile in the United States to community, the one that stands out, so to speak, with very little dissent as to its "correctness," or its validity and moral righteousness, is the time honored tradition of keeping the record of juveniles confidential. We say this is a tradition because it is long standing and, for the most part, seemingly inviolable. There are exceptions of course, but they are rare. One has only to peruse the daily tabloids to note that stories about misdeeds of juveniles always omit the identifying name and other pertinent information that would lead to identification. Often it appears mysterious at best, ludicrous at worst, when several juveniles are written about in terms of some delinquency crime or deviant act, and all those older than seventeen--the usual point of demarcation between juvenile and adult status-- are clearly identified while those younger -- of Juvenile Court jurisdictional age -- are referred to in the most oblique of terms: alleged delinquent is the most popular.

It is our purpose here to challenge this tradition. The very least that can be done in juvenile justice is to open for dialogue--investigation and research-- the whole problem. In the past several decades the use of publicity has been gaining momentum for adult offenders; this means anyone over juvenile age status -- seventeen in most localities and jurisdictions.

We know of several communities that have instituted arrangements with the press to print the names of drunk driving offenders. Our superficial impression is that it does appear to diminish these types of offenses. Other communities, such as Joliet, Illinois have in the past instituted the practice of arresting and publicizing the names and identifying information of "Johns" caught-up in vice sweeps where young female prostitutes have been gathered in large numbers. Again, there appears to be some payoff in reduced vice in the communities. Critics argue, not of course without some justification, that what happens is merely to disperse the deviant activities to other communities. The extent of this latter dispersion, with all of its ramifications has never been fully documented and analyzed. Though the argument appears plausible, it is fully conjectural.

That the time honored tradition of confidentiality is operative can be seen in two interesting cases. One involved the late Louis Wirth, who we referred to previously. Some while ago there was a public housing authority project built on Chicago's far south side. Following World War II it was one of the first of a number of projects designed especially for occupancy by the urban underclass; this meant, for the most part, a majority black population. If the planners, architects and policy implementers had wanted urban confrontation -- which they did not of course -- then they picked a community where it was assured. The project was immediately adjacent, abutting a large white, Polish ethnic enclave. What followed was racial violence of all sorts. The police of Chicago cordoned off the whole area, about one square mile of the city, where autos were stopped and/or diverted from entering the area. Whole squads of patrol police were brought in on shifts to try to maintain order. This lasted for several months.

It was at this time, during the Spring/Summer of 1951, that Professor Wirth told a graduate seminar at the University of Chicago that he was censoring the inflammatory press stories concerning both black and white juveniles and adults who were involved in "gang" style mayhem in This community. We doubt seriously that a Professor would now, in 1993, be in a position to oversee public information as was the case then -- forty years ago. Most agreed then, and we believe it would still be the case, that the public interest was best served by such censorship. The point we make here is that confidentiality was not the purpose of the protection of individuals as much as it was for the purpose of community interest. We would hope that a responsible press -- the Fourth Estate -- would oversee and police their own reporting. Such confidence in the Press is not always vindicated, as we will address later.

It was not for the purpose of individual rehabilitation that Louis Wirth was involved in censorship. Confidentiality of information is never simple. Sometimes the public interest is at stake, as in the above. Wirth was able to hold back from the press whole stores that were concluded to be inflammatory. He was deleting aggregate data, names of gang and groups, and his concerns did not touch upon individual alleged delinquents as such.

Another story addressing the issue of confidentiality involved an off duty policeman who was charged with the deliberate homicide of two youths. Actually the officer was on assignment to the States Attorney's office. This is the Chief Prosecutor for the County, and police assignments to this office are generally considered lucrative political attachments. The officer assigned to this duty had what is known in police jargon as a Rabbi, a sponsor with considerable clout; his outside civilian political sponsor had influence.

The officer was accused of killing two young males in their late teens/early twenties; the youths were Hispanic and the officer was Italian. At the first investigation and subsequent hearing, the press had concluded there was a "cover-up" of the facts in the case. Like any other profession or work association, the police had gathered around their accused colleague. The Patrolmen's Association and other police affiliates gathered around him (figuratively),... until the evidence was brought to light that the youths were both shot in the head, from behind, at close range. Powder burns were in evidence. A special prosecutor was named, the officer was indicted by a Grand Jury, and he was subsequently convicted of murder.

The interesting part of the story for purposes of understanding confidentiality was that the officer had a juvenile record. The Prosecution in the homicide case had wanted to get at this record in order to cast doubt on his character. After all, there were no witnesses to the killings. The Judge of the Juvenile Court personally withdrew the Juvenile Court file to see that the accused's juvenile record was not used in an adult, Criminal Court hearing. Here we would agree that in the interest of what we know as *due process*, confidentiality of juvenile delinquency information as it pertains to an individual's civil rights must be maintained. The Judge, in our opinion, acted correctly.

We see two cases where we totally agree that confidentiality must be maintained: one in the public interest over inflammatory information that can lead to violence (some interest in copy-cat crime, serial murders and such would obviously fit here); and another in our judicial system, where legal nuance, precedence, and opinion foster civil liberties by way of *due process*.

What we do urge is rethinking of the use of a generalized confidentiality; the kind of confidentiality that is reactive in knee-jerk fashion. In the past confidentiality has been invoked based on the claim that children have a right to protection from public scrutiny; that disclosure of detrimental information, in-and-by-itself, would do harm. The labeling school more than any other approach to rehabilitating delinquents calls attention to the adverse effects of publicity on the offender. It is taken as an axiom of faith that *if* the juveniles record becomes public knowledge, he will take on that role that has been assigned him by his own record being made public. There is a little bit of tautology here; circular reasoning shows through. First, the juvenile commits an offense, and then in making the offense public, he becomes that which he was! But we assume that before the information was made public, he didn't ascribe to or know who or what he was supposed to be! Only after public identification was the role solidified. We do think this theoretical exercise needs some attention. More will be said of the-so-called labeling school of thought later.

We do believe it is time to rethink the potential positive effects that selectively reducing, or eliminating the confidential nature of juvenile cases might bring about. Indeed the conflict theorists are not totally wrong in their observation that much of the case for confidentiality was for the practitioners in corrections; what they do, how they accomplish their jobs, without public knowledge, can only lead to a lack of accountability. We are not in agreement with the radicals who charge that confidentiality is only the means of a cover-up of inadequate at the least, and irresponsible at the most, services to juveniles. The charge that confidentiality is the handmaiden of the incompetent care-giver is an indictment of the system, and although we are not in agreement with it,...sometimes it is true. If anything, the possible charge that confidentiality can be a cloak for the incompetent practitioner opens up the possibility of reviewing the positive effects publicity might have in reducing the social problems of delinquency. To merely "stand on a pedestal," pontificating about the rights of the juvenile to privacy, etc., can be suspect.

Recently a few authors have taken aim at this problem of confidentiality as we see it. Interestingly some of the most novel considerations have been generated from outside the United States. Perhaps this is because in addressing how to moderate this traditional imperative, how to publicize delinquent transgressions as well as other forms of deviance, the liberal establishment and particularly the professoriate, have the same problem here that exists for the study of racial distribution as it relates to delinquency:

> ...to discuss any aspect of race and crime is automatically to give offense and to arouse anger. Thus, the subject has been almost taboo--an 'elephant in the room' whose presence one dared not mention.
> (Shireman and Reamer 1986: 29)

To even think about "taking away the basic right" of confidentiality from juveniles puts liberal credentials "in hock."

Braithwaite and Pettit, two social scientists from Australia have put forward a rather interesting theory on the use of *shameing* and *affirmation*: "... an individual is related to his community by rituals of shame and affirmation: the former provides both a dis-incentive for anti-social behavior and a means of public atonement; the latter offers the possibility of reintegrating the repentant criminal into the larger society." (*Washington Post* 10/28/90:C3;1)

What is needed, according to these authors, is repentance *and* forgiveness in order to reintegrate the deviant into our ways of life. They look to shame as happening, from the disapproving glance of authority, on through various forms of sarcasm, reproachment and public humiliation. They are careful to note what they are talking about is a type of "reintegrative shaming," always looking forward to the errant's return to grace. Unlike the early Christian ritual of *anathema* ("be ye eternally dammed"), Braithwaite and Pettit's advice seems to have intriguing points to consider.

As a further consideration on the confidentiality tradition within the juvenile justice system, let us add, if we have not already, that we urge dialogue on how to best use public information in the child's interest. We are, after all, still adherents to the rehabilitative model; sometimes shaken a bit with the "nothing works" doctrine, but none-the-less committed to an idea that human beings can uplift themselves in this life; and if others can help, so much the better.

Care must be taken here. We would not want to underestimate at all the potential for harm that disclosure of information, that humiliating persons might have. Braithwaite cautions against the kind of derogation of others that he refers to as "disintegrative shaming." To be sure, the American criminal justice system must be on guard against humiliation of clients--inmates, parolees, probationers and others. Braithwaite does differentiate between "integrative shaming" and humiliation, which he would regard as disintegrative and not serving the goal of community well-being. Perhaps Braithwaite's notion of humiliating others is closest to that observation of Professor Donald Taft, where he pointed out the most debilitating aspect of prison life to be the *condescension* of staff toward inmates; to this extent we are in agreement.

We are confident that the social scientists have progressed to a point where they will be able to implement some of their considerable understandings; one has only to reminisce the past as it relates to juvenile offenders to know how far we have come. When reading the social science literature, this point is often overlooked.

The concept of deterrence has two meanings: specific deterrence and general deterrence. The former has to do with an individual changing in reaction to perceived threat. The latter has to do with the constraint of others by way of example; seeing someone punished deters would-be deviants. General deterrence, by definition then, *must* have publicity. (Fisse and Braithwaite 1983)

In some delinquency control assessments, *containment* theory depends on the two-pronged factor of inner and outer containment. Inner containment is thought to be the individual living up to *personal* constraints, while outer containment depends on the strength of values and codes of community conduct to control the individual. Inner containment, therefore, is more closely related to specific deterrence while outer containment and general deterrence have more affinity. Community values and codes must be known and publicized in order to work.

When sociologists considered the self-fulfilling prophecy, originally introduced several decades ago by Merton, they mostly concentrated on that aspect of this definition that was called the *positive Pygmalion*; this is best thought of as the individual living up to the positive expectations of others. Negative expectations were to be avoided as they were thought to lead to the self-fulfilled debasement   of the person.   Only lately have sociologists even mentioned the *Galitea* effect, intended to convey the idea that individuals can and do self-fulfill their own private expectations.

Again, on the role of confidentiality in juvenile cases, we think that juveniles in a community have their own ways of knowing, of getting information when others, their rivals, and their peers get into trouble with the law. Often the information is severely distorted. One would have to wonder if publicity given in a straight-forward manner would not be beneficial to everyone concerned, especially when compared to the kind of information that is passed around "street-wise."

And how do we expect that young people will come to know community standards, values, sanctions, and even the law except through publicity? Can anyone seriously suggest *Civics* classes in Junior or Senior High? Anyone who has worked the streets as a probation or parole worker with juveniles can attest to the fantastic lack of understandings that exist out there. So many of pre-adjudicated and alleged delinquents used to ask "...is *that* illegal?" (One of the authors remembers young juveniles asking this question for rape, auto larceny,...you name it). Such social and legal *naivete* had led to the "operating room" humour that the only thing around the Court that was illegal was a bird, ...the ill Eagle!

Concerning Social Relations of Juvenile Delinquents:

Institutional living: During the "heyday" of those years when the liberal rehabilitative model was operational and vigorous, up to the nineteen-sixties, two central themes headed the list for practitioners in what is now the juvenile justice field: to treat clients well and to maintain the best semblance of order and civility possible. This would be true both in and out of institutional living arrangements but it would appear more obvious--indeed more imperative-- at correctional facilities.   Later critics argued, with reasoned plausibility, that this was not enough to bring about rehabilitative change in individuals. The whole of rehabilitation became questioned in a supposed unjust society where rich and poor were becoming increasingly divided.   Now that correctional practice is plagued by both political and professional criticism that "nothing works" programmatically to rehabilitate offenders, the themes of treating well and maintaining civility are argued mostly in terms of cost effectiveness.

We were recently surprised and amused at the study findings of the

Center for the Study of Youth Policy of the University of Michigan. In 1989 Center staff, together with Nebraska legislators and institutional employees, conducted an investigation at two Youth Development Centers (Kearney and Geneva, Nebraska.) The purpose of the study was to outline alternatives to incarceration. On site observations indicated that "...no serious incidents have occurred (which) raises questions about the population housed at Kearney." (*Criminal Justice Newsletter*, June 15 1990). And again, the investigators assert that "...thepleasant environment at Geneva suggests the same paradox a visitor encounters at Kearney: if youths in the YDC are so well behaved, so trouble free, why is it necessary to place them in such a controlled setting?" (*ibid*)

The conclusion was drawn that since everything was going so well, that since a state of civility existed, that *something must be wrong!* Good grief! We would wonder why the institutional staff and legislators who bought this study (half million dollars) were not incensed. Instead, two Juvenile Court Judges agreed, apologizing that there weren't any alternatives. We do not argue that other alternatives, particularly community based programs ought be sought. What we do object to is the point that an institutional goal of civility, having been met, is used as evidence of failure. One would have to ask the conclusion of the study team *if* pandemonium had been witnessed. Probably the same conclusion, that the inmate population doesn't belong there.

We recently had occasion to be at one of the many conferences that go on in the United States, addressing the problems of institutional confinement. At the opening banquet when the few experts were addressing the major issues of today, a young black lady, in her late thirties, whispered "...they don't know; they haven't been there." Our conversation then, was to recount our shared experiences in institutional correctional settings. She had been a correctional social service worker in a closed institutional setting. Our point here is that we are not sure reasonable assessments on institutional living can be made by people who have not been there. More will be said of this later.

One of the goals of operating a correctional facility has been to keep control in the hands of the staff. A case can be made that, after all, the staff is getting paid to run the operation. An "inmate run institution" is perhaps the most severe criticism of the chief administrator. In recent years much has been made of involving the client population in decision making. In our democratic, western, civilized society, this goal of inmate involvement is difficult to argue against. To make it happen, involvement, without it being on the one hand a sham, and on the other, an inmate run place surely tests the mettle of the most competent of staff.

Staff at correctional institutions are always aware of the kinds of roles that inmates bring with them. In the case of juveniles having gang backgrounds this can be important for the appropriate running of a facility. A delinquent gang has the potential of super-imposing an organizational structure on an institutional setting. We're not sure how to read Yablonsky on this; he does define the delinquent gang to be a "near group." (1962). Probably, the *near group* concept is very close to how we feel about the social role concept: both are fragile, transitory, and relatively short lived. For that short period of time that a delinquent gang asserts itself, however, it is very real. It is for this reason that institutional staff would attempt to see that the gang does not materialize as a social entity while in confinement. It poses too much threat to other inmates and the total operation. Civility becomes threatened.

We know that in the past, delinquent gangs were the focus of attention where programs were aimed at redirecting their energies, organizational structures and goals. The term indigenous leadership[6] meant that gangs had their own hierarchy. Attempts were made to work toward positive community goals by enlisting and co-opting this indigenous elite. Yablonsky refers to the various gangs that he had worked with; some even developed a resentment at *not* having an assigned caseworker. Our impression is that it is next to impossible to adequately redirect delinquent gang activities *as a group*. Yablonsky would agree here; his recommendation would be to "peel off the marginal members." (1962:249-54) He likens the process to "stripping the artichoke." (*ibid*: 290) By extension then, working with the delinquent gang as a unit would not appear profitable.

We argue in this monograph that our attention ought be focused on the social relations of young people that are delinquency related. Except in a very few instances, the social role concept, as if it applied to a vast array of normative prescriptions, sanctions, status arrangements and the like, really is not the case. There are *a few cases* though, where the social role does apply. Yablonsky identified the gang leader as a role type. For him, the gang leader was the really weird, sociopathic individual who was constantly attempting to validate his own existence, usually violently. We have witnessed a few of these persons over the years; indeed, our only quibble is that they were *not* the indigenous leader types, but rather something else. Gangs, not all but some, seemed sometimes to have a very unusual member, more prone to violence for the sake of violence. These individuals had to be identified and isolated. It is very probable that we know so little about them as a type because of their very violent nature. They are quite dangerous. Their very existence is more impressionistic than empirically verifiable.

While in custodial situations, juveniles do not really take on social roles, unless one would consider the various tasks assigned to be role performances.[7]   Such an interpretation would do serious injustice to the concept of role. However, there are many, many social relations that occur. Matza has considered the interaction of delinquents in a kind of verbal sparring that goes on; he has named this "sounding." (1964: 42-44) Probably every social worker has witnessed the situation where boys verbally "spar" around with each other. The object of this kind of game, although it can quickly escalate into a fight, seems to be a kind of one-upmanship.

Actually, it has parallels in the adult world. The differences usually are apparent. More often than not delinquents start out with verbal defamation. And again, this is often aimed at the sparring partner's mother. This probably is thought to bring about the most of confrontation and reaction. Usually it works. As indicated, the confrontation isn't *supposed* to end in violence. That it does really attests to the lack of what in the adult world would be maturity. Civility, good manners, and getting along with others has not been learned.[8]

Other kinds of social relations take place. Most institutional staff are aware of the dialogues that go on between themselves and the inmates. One social worker that we referred to previously, the thirty-ish black social worker at the conference, had summed up much of the kind of social relations between staff and inmates when she observed: "they stay awake nights thinking of things to say, games to play with me."

We have not said much of female populations in confinement. Several authors have written about the differences between boys and girls in custody. We would agree with Bortner (1982 Ch.10) that staff generally would prefer to work with the male populations. Most of the kinds of references we have to female populations seem overly impressionistic. Gibbons (1976) calls much of the problems that are endemic for girls as originating from an "under the roof culture." By this he means that the original problem stems from the home, the relations between child and parents. Between Gibbon's first edition (1970) and his most recent fifth (1991) the concern and focus on female juvenile offenders has shrunk. Whole chapters were devoted in earlier editions while the latest has a scant four pages. The considerations   of Trojanowicz and Morash for the female offender are also sparse and spread through-out their text. (1987) A perusal of delinquency texts will reveal much the same. Bartollas' text (1990) has one of the better and more detailed accountings of female delinquency theory and description, although it too co-mingles the description and analysis with more general concerns. This is not exactly criticism: it is an observation as to the way it is. The professionals and experts in delinquency have concentrated more on other aspects, particularly the male involvement.

A final point we will make on institutional populations is that on overcrowding. This seems to be a problem that is always with us. Current, recent, and far in the past literature notes constantly make reference to it. Institutional administrators are aware of this as a problem and all speak against it. On the other hand, can we consider institutional population size in terms of minimum, maximum, optimum?

The thrust today as in the past is to have goals of confinement *only* for those juvenile most in *need* of this type of control. Confinement should be for those that pose risk to themselves and/or the community. A strong case could be made however, that an institution populated with some of the most severely troubled youngsters, would be extremely difficult in which to maintain a semblance of order and civility. It can be done, but what would it be from the standpoint of the inmates? Most detention facility staff know what it is like at an institution over Christmas and Easter holidays. Judges of Juvenile Courts, eager to conform to the spirit of these holidays, empty out the confinement places of most all that are reasonable risks. The population that is left is often without the stabilizing influence of children with less severe problems. This is hardly a reason for holding youngsters. But it does occur to staff that things go more smoothly when populations have representatives with less severe emotional and social impairments.

In the next chapter we want to address some of the many thoughts that have been given over the years as to how and why youngsters do what they do. Most delinquency texts have a number of chapters that are referred to as the theory part of our understandings and information. For simplicity we refer to this as the plot.

ENDNOTES FOR CHAPTER THREE

1. Most dictionaries define protagonist as the central or lead character in a play. Roget's thesaurus quite correctly draws attention to the dark side of this role; another connotation: the first tragedian. We would liken our reference to delinquent as protagonist to be as Shakespeare developed the characters of the young Prince Hamlet, or the dark prince, Othello; our fascination is riveted, but affection, tenderness, and fondness are not part of the equation.

2. Professor Len Pecilunas is retired from Northern Illinois University at DeKalb. His doctoral dissertation (Florida State University, Tallahassee, 1965) avoided the kind of direct definition of delinquency that so often gets the researcher in trouble: in the effort to be objective, attention is focused upon the impossibility of language exactness.

3. One of the first employees of the rodent control function of the city of Chicago was a former child attendant of the juvenile correctional facility, Mr. Fred Jeske. He was one of those few individuals who brought considerable compassion and service to his position. Once again we witnessed a job change that was welcomed by an individual but a cheerless event for an institution.

4. Murder, homicide, manslaughter, all connote slightly different meanings. Second degree murder would encompass the killing of another human as a by-product of the commission of a felony. A felony is a legally defined transgression of State statute. First degree murder denotes the specific intention to kill a particular human. Confessions to authorities can be described as if on a continuum: at the one extreme the person confessing in reality accedes to facts already known; at the other extreme the person confesses freely, of his own volition, to facts hitherto unknown. This latter suffers from a catch-22: if a person freely confesses intent, to *mens rea* (a guilty mind) under the law, he must be of unsound mind as he is *not* acting in his own best interest. If he does not confess openly and freely, can his silence, which is guaranteed by the United States Constitution, be construed as guilt? Not so in western cultural jurisprudence. However, eastern cultural legal tradition and perspective allows for *adverse inference* by authorities when silence is invoked. This point has gotten several of american youth in serious difficulty when they were adjudicated in jurisdictions like Turkey, Russia, and even Mexico. Even Scotland bases its jurisprudence on Roman tradition, which is different in respects from the English law tradition and ours.

Juvenile courts in the United States *used to be* much more like the eastern cultural tradition and jurisprudence.

5. Referral to a juvenile court or detention facility results in some type of classification of the individual referred. The breakdown of delinquency into offence categories is interesting. The resulting typologies logically delineate the many ways a juvenile can get into trouble and come to the attention of authorities. An exhaustive taxonomy *always* results in a final category of "*all other.*" This category is left open to particular offenses being recorded, such as *attempted poisoning*.

This category, while not the most useful, is perhaps the most interesting.

6. During the Johnson administration of the 1960's, much effort was made to reach out to troubled youth of our inner cities. Public and private agencies began to try to redirect identified youth toward more productive lives. Those were the days of outreach and detached worker influence. The obvious way to reach the large underclass was to first concentrate and work with the indigenous leadership of youth groups, gangs, or whatever they were. There was mixed success in this venture. At times the authorities were simply taken, finessed by such leaders.

7. David Dressler was an academic who had been a parole chief. He has described and detailed types of criminals within institutional confinement. He has also added to the literature, describing a number of role performances in the world of crime. There is no similar undertaking for juveniles in delinquency.

8. One of the very best descriptions of juveniles taking their measure of one another is in Matza's *Delinquency and Drift.* (1964) He calls it *sounding*.

4
The Plot

In this chapter we will address some of the concerns about explaining the social problem of delinquency. All of the textbooks, not only in delinquency, but also in criminology and the other areas of the sociology of deviance, abnormal psychology, clinical sociology/psychology, social psychology, and so forth seem remarkably similar in their treatment of "cause." In science we prefer not to deal directly with causative factors. Instead we focus on what is termed the independent variable, ...that variable, though unaffected by, affects a dependent variable.

Explanations of delinquency and other deviant human activity are generally grouped under three umbrellas: biology; psychology; sociology. Sometimes these are stated differently; sometimes they are further subdivided; almost always they are referred to as theory. Even when it is obvious that the topic being discussed is not theory, but rather a treatment approach, or a set of observations, the invocation of a theoretical stance is intoned.

There are many good books to which the reader may turn to learn of the wide array of theories--explanations--of delinquency. It is not our purpose here to add yet another taxonomy with brief overviews and criticisms. Rather we would prefer to set down some of our more general concerns, observations and recommendations.

It was stated above that some of what passes for theory is in reality something else. This does not demean the work of others. But it is to say that, by analogy, it is no more an explanation of time by pointing to a clock than it is to observe some of the correlates of delinquency. In the past, many, many variables have been found to be co-related. All sorts of physical factors, social factors, demographic and ecological factors have been put forward and analyzed.

Many of the readers will recall that upon being introduced to the scientific method, the first of several steps is the testing of hypothetical relationships. The hypothesis became the building block(s) of theory. More general theory would follow. Student dissatisfaction with this approach often follows when it becomes obvious that no matter how many specific variables can be tested, there always seemed to be an endless array of others. New variables are hypothesized to be related. Old variables are subdivided or rearranged. As a result it seems that many authors go directly to more far reaching explanations of deviant behavior.

The one thing that theory ought *not* to do is to introduce a further liability. We ought to better understand following explanations, rather than otherwise. We are not sure this is the case as a result of the many explanations of crime and delinquency that have been put forward. Some of the explanations compete with one another. Biology and heredity are often seen as opposites to psychology and learning theory. Labeling theory appears opposite the predilection of education and teaching to early identify academic and social problems. And, as many explanations do well in amassing evidence "proving" a hypothetical relationship, often ignored is the point that for an independent variable to be accepted as affecting the dependent variable of delinquency, the unstated non-delinquent is part of the equation. This cannot always be answered by the use of controlled variables, adequately or inadequately applied.

Sometimes it's like getting five hundred people together and having them flip coins to see which ones get heads. If you then have those that turned up heads flip again, and again repeat the game...after about six flips of the coin by the constant remaining "winners," you'll end up with about a dozen persons. All of these have flipped six consecutive heads! It should *not* be the task of science to investigate the social and psychological backgrounds of these individuals to determine their predilection to winning! Such would be preposterous.[1]

Various explanations of delinquency seem to come and go over time. It is in the pejorative sense that theory is sometimes described as if a "fad." And we are not comfortable with this assessment, even when there is some obvious truth to it. So we often advise students as newcomers to the field of corrections to learn a little of all the theoretical positions described in the literature, ...but to become versed, to know really well one of their choosing. Containment theory is often suggested for its ease of understanding. It is equally adaptable to future work situations. Focusing as it does on inner controls of the personality and coupled with outer controls of community constraints it offers good advice in its applicability to social histories. And it is to the social/personal history that many newcomers to the field will devote their efforts. Social workers quickly come to understand that their competence and industry is most often judged by their written reports. "Put it in writing" has become more than the casual recommendation to new staff.

Both inner strengths/weaknesses of the individual plus the other strengths/weakness of community organization and cohesion can aptly be described with adjectives. Exuberant and lethargic, abundance of resource, poverty of human interaction, openness and paranoia, institutional variety, commitment to charity, ...all become the words and tools of containment theory. And best still is the ease with which others understand what is being portrayed and described. Perhaps this was part of the reason the guest speaker to the delinquency class referred to earlier had concluded that English classes, particularly rhetoric and composition, were of such value after graduation.

For the most part students easily understand and accept a single explanatory stance. This is what is most often called *labeling theory*. The public itself appears to have heard of it. Judges, police, the layman, all have a general idea of what it is about. But as Wheeler and Cottrell pointed (1966) out, it really isn't theory. Although these two writers accept its fundamental premise that labeling is precarious, and we ought not involve juveniles in the juvenile justice apparatus 'willy-nilly,'they do point out that the labeling as an explanation of delinquency is nothing more, and we would add nothing less, than the observation that people react as they are treated. In sociology this observation has been around for a long time. One has only to mention Cooley's "looking glass self" to attest to the time honored prescription. (Bierstedt 1974: 195-202) People behave as they are expected; and they react as they perceive others expect them to react. But not always. It is this latter point and observation that most seriously troubles the practitioners in the field of corrections. Some people simply don't conform to expectations!

Quite aside from what we consider to be the over simplistic reliance on labeling theory, and we would prefer to call it the labeling school because it represents a group of adherents, is the point that is often made by those in teaching. Elementary school teachers go through formal training, usually in schools and colleges of education. One of the first things they learn about is the early identification of problems. They are taught to be on the lookout for suspected learning disabilities as well as physical impairment. More recently the mass media has given vivid accounts of child abuse uncovered in the classroom. Pre-school and nursery care centers are also places where the identification of problems stemming from the home have been reported recently. And with some degree of righteousness, the public appears satisfied with the process of an early identification of problems. No one can condone child abuse and molestation.

But what of early identification of other problems? Delinquency proneness for instance? We are not convinced that knowledge and identification of potential problems are inherently bad. It is the use to which knowledge is put that will make the difference. Certainly there have been an abundance of cases that were sent through the juvenile justice pipeline early in this century, and on up until the mid-1970's that should have been diverted or, better still, dismissed. As to the "net-widening" that resulted in additional cases being officially handled as a result of diversion programs of the late '70's' and early '80's, common sense and propriety should have led to the conclusion that they would have been better off left alone and not "labeled."

But for an increasingly large number of juveniles who have become involved in serious delinquent behavior, we feel that NOT to label, NOT to adjudicate, NOT to give our attention is a serious mistake. As we noted in the previous chapter, the roles people play in life are numerous and transitory; that they are also fragile, as noted by Banton (*ibid.* 1965) would lend substance to our inference that the labeling of juveniles as delinquent is far less permanent and damaging than is suggested by the labeling school. We are in reality addressing simple social relationships that do not have the permanence of social role systems.

Then too, a case could be made to show that where the label really counts, in the peer group, in the family, and in the community, the label of delinquent, however it is called, already exists prior to police, court, school and/or agency contact. To defer from official contact for many cases is, to put it bluntly and as the juveniles themselves would, "...a cop-out." At times one would wonder along with the conflict theorists and radical sociologists if the labeling school advocates are not really looking to lowered taxes through advocating less official action. It is a conservative goal to have less government. It is surprising that this particular point has not been raised before by the liberal press. The reader is directed to Shireman and Reaman's critique of labeling. These authors contend that authorities already "...are vigorous in thrusting delinquents *out* of the system (and that they are frequently subjected to severe public criticism as a result)" (*ibid.* p.50)

Enough said concerning labeling. Quite another way of explaining delinquency that enjoyed respect and longevity in the correctional field was psychoanalysis. It was probably not until the 1960's that this theoretical perspective began to be put on the back burner so to speak. From the earliest part of this century it dominated agency and court practice. There was a time shortly after World War II that the up-and-coming career oriented person would opt for personal psychoanalysis after obtaining formal academic credentials. This often took a year or even two years time; personal analysis became another and perceived more commanding credential for which to practice rehabilitating others. The Franz Alexander School of Psychoanalysis in Chicago was one of the places to which practitioners turned. Going through analysis became a kind of additional graduate training.

Psychoanalytic theory is the oldest to which modern practice of rehabilitation has turned. The impressive thing about this theory is its tightly woven precepts, concepts, inferences, conclusions and implications; not so impressive are its empirical verifications. It takes the proverbial leap of faith to go from theory to reality. That which seems so logical, so reasonable an explanation based on hypotheses derived from the theory is found wanting when put to the empirical test of verification: where is the evidence? Such criticism is bound to anger some. We would leave it for argument at another time, another place.

There are many insights, though, that psychoanalysis can provide for us. (Lindzey 1954: Ch.4) Three concepts come to mind: transference; counter-transference; rationalization.

Transference as a concept means that a client eventually displaces pent-up emotional feelings onto the practitioner. Counter-transference is the opposite: it means that the practitioner eventually transfers his emotional feelings onto the client.

Working in Corrections, and for that matter in any field with people who have problems, it is wise to know of these two concepts. The tabloids of recent years are replete with sexual *peccadillos* of errant practitioners. Even where outrageous and obviously unethical behavior is avoided, close personal involvement of practitioner-client ought be steadfastly avoided. This is why we urge an abundance of empathy and little sympathy. We know of too many instances where transference and counter-transference, as psychoanalytic concepts, become a reality and jeopardized all that was involved: relationships, careers, families, common sense. The call for people to work in Corrections that are "not the nine-to-fivers," should be accompanied by special *caveats* about this mental process. (see Chapter Two)

The other concept that is most useful in corrections and comes to us from psychoanalysis is that of rationalization. What it means is that a person puts forward his best case for his actions. He presents himself verbally by adjusting and re-adjusting the story of his behavior. Usually connoted by rationalization is the idea that the person who is rationalizing is making it all "sound better" than it is in reality. All of this is not new to sociology. Goffman's work is well known, but perhaps his paperback on "Presentation of Self in Everyday Life," is the most appreciated. (1959) In this monograph Goffman meticulously unravels the efforts at self protection. The concept of self was an early pre-occupation for sociologists. It always took on more importance in an understanding of human dignity than did the concept of role. If the labeling school had paid more attention to this aspect--the self--we might have had to conclude that they were on to something. The reciprocity of delinquency and self-esteem now appears an enigma or catch-22. Raising levels of self-esteem may in some cases lower delinquency proneness, but becoming delinquent can result in positive self conceptualization. (Rosenberg, Schooler, and Schoenbach 1989)

Closely related to rationalization is what David Matza calls the "social work ethic." It is different in that it is the practitioner who helps provide socially acceptable excuses for behavior. He acts as an accomplice.

Knowing about these psychoanalytic concepts may not be enough to completely prevent undesirable and unwarranted problems. But at least it is a start. Students especially need to be told about possible encounters. They should even be told that to prevent their early career burn-out, they should be careful about offering after-hour counseling to clients; take care how widespread the home phone number is given out.

Yet another pervasive explanation and way of handling delinquency has been that of behavioralism. This particular theory, together with its many facets, appears to go through phases. It has been kind of "off-again, on again" throughout the past several decades. Actually, behavioralism owes its formal underpinning to the much earlier stimulus-response theory of the laboratory psychologists. Although the original founder of the behavioral school was Watson, behavioralism as a respectable discipline is conjured up by the memory of Pavlov. (Lindzey 1954:Ch.2) Indeed it is reasonably accurate to speak of behavioralism as Pavlovian.   Some of the behavioral school adherents might be uneasy with the word "Pavlovian" noting its pejorative reference to animal conditioning; but perhaps they should not stray too far from the findings associated with laboratory experiment. Behavioral therapy is for the most part individualized. (Hollin 1990: 51-54) The difficulty in monitoring individual progress and sustained effects is obvious. Still, further work in this area would be called for.

Early on, dating back several decades, many places of incarceration seeking to rehabilitate juveniles used the most obvious operations of behavior: reward and punishment; the carrot and the stick. While the employment of rewards to stimulate desired behavior seemed most reasonable, giving extra privileges like time off for movies, home visits, even money rewards, the use of punishment seemed to fall apart. On questioning any director of places where behavioralism is the model, the usual point is made that the negative part of the equation, punishment, is the withholding of rewards. This appears kind of empty. Is it long before the young delinquent, the clients in correction, "see through," this arrangement? It is understandable in our society and culture that we are reluctant to make punishment meaningful. But we do have a difficult time in wondering how to make behavioralism as a model work.

Some institutions have employed "chits,"a kind of in-house money that can be earned as reward. The adult system has long used "good time" as a bargaining chip for acceptable behavior. But in trying to provide decent human surroundings, in treating persons "well," where are the negative incentives? Most recently two authors (Cullen and Gilbert 1982) noted that the rehabilitation model itself was predicated on the idea of treating people "well,"and that in and by itself, this would rehabilitate. Liberals who so long held to this tenet of faith now draw attention to treating clients "well"because it is cheaper! They have yet to sell this to a conservatively hostile public.

There are many other theoretical positions and explanations of human behavior. In trying to reform, retrain, rehabilitate delinquent youth, many models of treatment have been tried. As far as the theoretical stance would go for various treatment approaches, most are overlapping and are not mutually exclusive. Eclecticism is quite evident. Often times there is a kind of smorgasbord visible in the treatment process. Biological treatment programs through the use of the many modern (and recent) "wonder drugs" go hand-in-hand with sociological and psychological approaches. There used to be the story when the "wonder drugs" first appeared in Corrections that what really happened when the doctor ordered these miracle drugs was that he immediately sat down and "wondered" what would happen!

There is something about the use of many approaches, many theories --all at the same time-- that offend our sensibilities. Social Science Methodology instructs against mixing theory together. And yet in practice it is openly evident that jumping around in theory goes on. If you would watch young potential delinquents being counseled, and we have, you would notice that the practitioner often "jumps" from one theoretical stance to another. We neither want to over emphasize this, nor to especially criticize; we do want to warn of the implications of such eclecticism. Confusion is the least unacceptable   consequence: misunderstanding,   misinterpretation   and misdiagnosis are far more serious.

Social/psychological concerns are often wedded to psychiatric theory. Transactional analysis would typify this. (Nicholson 1970: 29-39) The earlier press had correctly identified Eric Berne's (1964) treatment approaches as a kind of "pop psychoanalysis."[2] It caught on as a way to help people try to solve some of their problems.   Fashioned after models of psychoanalytic insights, it was easy to understand and clients could get into it, interacting with others and the practitioner.   We know of Marriage Counselors who travelled to California in the early 1970's to become specially trained in "T.A.," as it was known.

Much good can be said about this method of helping people.   Like Carl Roger's client centered therapy of the late 1940's-early 1950's, T.A. depends much on the assumption that persons with problems, once they know and understand, once they come to cognitive grips with their problems, are then well on the road to being rehabilitated.   More than a few helping strategies   whether   founded   on eclecticism   or theory depend   on this assumption.   We urge extreme caution here; a strong case can be made that knowing one's problems is not enough. On the other hand, we might hasten to add that *understanding* is necessary.   The older social science textbooks used to point to the "necessary, but insufficient" variables in explanations of behavior.   Perhaps in this sense T.A. has the capacity to be helpful. Knowledge of one's problems can be gained in the interaction of client, practitioner, and others while "playing" Transactional Analysis.

This point of the assumption that knowledge of one's problems is insufficient to affect positive change should be well taken. It is a troubling criticism of the basic assumption.   Yet the criticism is there.   There is the anecdote of conventional wisdom from prisons, that if you want to get released early, act like a "real S.O.B."; really cause problems.   Then, when you're sure they've got the message, ...change; be good; be helpful. They'll think they "cured you" and you'll earn the release! Contrary-wise, if you come in acting good., ...they'll wonder why you're there. They'll hold you longer just to find out!

The above is of course full of the cynicism that is "supposed" to be so pervasive in places of incarceration. Donald Taft pointed to cynicism as one of the guiding ethics of prison life. So we do bring this up as a warning to be especially careful in depending on cognitive skills as they relate to rehabilitation.   We understand that today many of the "buzzwords" for changing offender populations have to do with education. Especially with the tremendous increase in problems associated with illicit drugs, education has been held out as the surest road to a cure. With the advent of increasing problems of teenage pregnancies, plus the medical problem of the Acquired Immune Deficiency Syndrome (AIDS), education in sexual matters seems at the top of most agenda. But knowledge itself must be accompanied by something else. We will address this more at length under another theoretical stance. This time from psychology.

We have been much impressed with the social psychologist's work on what is termed cognitive dissonance. (Festinger 1963) Sometimes this is referred to as an equilibrium model. Basically the explanation has to do with cognitive and affective perception. The meaning of dissonance is that of psychological unease, vague feelings that something is amiss, (e.g., misplacing your keys, eye glasses, etc., and not feeling comfortable until located). The opposite of dissonance is consonance, that is, feelings of well being, that all is right with the world. It is really the absence of dissonance.

This equilibrium model further suggests that we try to make "sense" of that which is perceived; perception comes to us by way of the physical senses (biological). Making "sense" of what is perceived is a cognitive skill. But as the theory goes, it is not "easy" to do so; most of our perceptions are, at the least, disparate -- that is, we must interpret them cognitively. The theory further states that unless and until we come to terms with the meaning involved in our perceptions, we will encounter dissonance -- an affective experience. Our inner well being is threatened, and we feel it through our sense of unease.

Numerous examples from everyday life can be cited here, from the misplaced trivial objects (keys, eye glasses), to the 'lost' car in the parking lot. Less than trivial are the cognitive perceptions of honesty, trustworthiness, loyalty and so forth. How do we reconcile meaning here when the "push and pull" of our society's norms tugs us in different directions? The theory has an assumption that the inner psyche cannot tolerate "too much" of long term dissonance. In effect we block out or disregard those disparate messages that prevent cognitive acceptance of the one "true" message.

Cognitive dissonance is much like Hegel's dialectic at some points. The reader might well remember the old "thesis -- antithesis = synthesis" model here. It addresses the notion that every idea has its opposite (antithesis); we are constantly reforming ideas and images of truth with new, acceptable, and accepted ideas (synthesis). (Neill 1956: 109-15)

We wonder why we have not seen attempts at application of cognitive dissonance to reform juvenile offenders. To be sure some aspects of the theory seem to be part of behavior modification. It is understood that some form of "mediation" occurs between the practitioner and client over the *meaning* of rewards in stimulus-stimulus response remedial situations. It is also equally understood that this application of behavior modification assumes the motivated, willing client. In corrections the unwilling, unmotivated client must be assumed. Here is where-in the problem lies.

We can think of ways to keep up the dissonance levels in individuals without resorting to harsh measures. If we could apply them to ideas of value like honesty, fair-play and even truth-telling, some advances in human interaction might well be realized. This would necessitate staff involvement and direction more-so than is commonly found. It would probably take the concerted attention of staff and client population.

We recently visited and toured the U.S. Marine Corps Brig at Quantico where it is believed rudimentary forms of the equilibrium model are in place. This we know is open to argument. But our observations were that the staff are able to get the attention of those confined. Outwardly at least, some degree of dissonance appears present. The population of inmates appeared to exhibit much less of an outward facade of confrontation, such as is the case in many of our places of confinement, like for instance San Quentin.

Also, during a decade of observing an In-take department of Chicago's detention facility, newly admitted, pre-adjudicated delinquents were observed. It was the general consensus among those who supervised, worked with, interviewed, and were generally responsible for incarcerated juveniles that there was an optimum time to detain. Too short (a minimum) and too long (a maximum) seemed to be ineffective. Twenty-four to thirty-six hours seemed to be an optimum time.[3]

What we are saying is that dissonance appeared in detainees during this period. Release before twenty-four hours (give-or-take) and detention after thirty-six seemed counter-productive; the juvenile reacted "as if" it were a game; during this very short period their actions at least evidenced dissonance. Although this is probably not appropriate for the recidivist and some others, like the violent offender, it would appear advantageous for the many. It's reminiscent of "scared straight" without the formalities of such a program. Caution would be urged here such that not all youngsters caught up in the net be detained; it isn't for all. Adequate discretion on the part of admitting staff would have to be maintained. Some localities have probation officers acting on a twenty-four hour basis evaluating the need of incarceration. They act as sort of "officer of the watch," ordering release or detention on the basis of fact, need, and law.

In the mid-1950's Albert Cohen (1955) wrote on the delinquent subculture of the juvenile gang. Later on, Yinger (1960) was to introduce the concept of the contra-culture; this was the description of a youthful delinquent gang that had turned mainstream society's values upside-down. Although social class backgrounds became key issues of Cohen's inquiry into delinquency, it was the idea of access to societal rewards that was central to his thesis.

Inquiry into delinquent gang activity has been a long term preoccupation in the correctional field. Thrasher first noted some of the positive socializing aspects of the gang. (Robison 1963: 121-22) However, much of the research and observations on gangs emphasized the predatory nature of the gang itself. Walter Miller (1950) with his emphasis on "focal concerns" is widely known; most of his attributes to the gang have such an emphasis. In spite of the inherent warning about the nature of the delinquent gang as expressed by way of these focal concerns (hedonistic, autonomous, "macho," always with the assumption of being "armed") the 1960's saw a renewed effort to control delinquent activity by working with the gangs. "Detached workers" were hired by both public and private agencies to mediate and work with gangs toward positive goals. Their workplace was in the community. The observation that gangs had an "indigenous" built-in leadership led to attempts to co-opt the direction of ganging. We have yet to hear of significant success stories. From time to time the media reports on some "gangs"in New York, and even in Milwaukee that have taken on a kind of vigilante function, policing the streets and subway trains. This activity -- a proper function of legitimate society through its legal arms -- would remind us of inmate run institutions. Although it can get the job done, ...we worry about the price to be paid, ...now or later.

When Cohen brought up the point of lack of legitimate access to societal goals, (*op.cit.* 1955) there was a renewed call for education reform. Especially for the lower social classes, the ways to alleviate the problems of delinquency were thought to be through the schools. Certainly, no one can argue that equal access to the tools of success are not worthwhile. Currently there is much debate and activity on how to reform the whole of the U.S. educational apparatus. We are heartened to see efforts at educational reform for its own sake. Cohen was generally correct in his thesis of an opportunity structure militating against the lower classes. In spite of criticism of the connection to delinquency gang formation, it seems self-evident that without an adequate opportunity structure and the educational means to achieve rewards, adolescents will turn to ways of achievement that are not in the interest of organized, civilized society.

Any Probation Officer or Case Worker with extensive field experience knows that material possessions are not the sole factor--including available, disposable income (or lack of it)-- nor perhaps even the necessary factor that is the key explanatory in predatory behavior. As intuition, the "alchemy of police experience," (Peter Benitez 1990) the suggestion of the subjective knowledge gained on the streets that tips off the knowledge of delinquency is useful; so also does that subjective knowledge inform us as to the limited explanatory value material possessions have for delinquency possessions. "I did it for the money," or because "I needed it," has to be re-interpreted. All too often we see that the delinquent already controls material possessions.

Cloward and Ohlin (1960) later added to the analysis of America's opportunity structure. Whereas Cohen had indicated that delinquent gang formation was a result of failed success in legitimate societal undertakings, these authors pointed out that in some important ways this did not always lead to delinquent gangs and violence. They suggested that in many cases it was not even opportune to become delinquent. Perhaps Cloward and Ohlin were taking a hint from containment theory, where the community description would be such that it was just not appropriate to engage in particular forms of deviant behavior.

There was a Police precinct just south of the University of Chicago that had an area where much was to behold in the way of social problems of prostitution, vice of all sorts, drugs, poverty, etc. Gang delinquency was not one of these problems, although by the early 1960's this had changed dramatically. There was the story of a police beat officer along the 63rd Street mainfare. He had the reputation of carrying four pistols (at least) and a horse riding crop. The story was that potential delinquents didn't come within miles of him. Incidentally he had the nickname of "Pistol Pete." He later was fired as a policeman. The story was that he had brought in one too many dead prisoners,... "trying to escape." Some of these stories are difficult to validate.

Concerning the State's Attorney's police officer of the late 1950's who was brought to trial for killing two young men "trying to escape" (see pp. 63-64); this occurred in the Chicago area immediately south of the Loop. Michael Moretti was later sent to the State Prison after a long trial by a special prosecutor. Apparently the two youths had given the officer a "hard time" when he sought to question them; while he was off-duty, one of the requirements of policing in Chicago at that time was to be armed--to carry a gun. This did not bode well for the two young men.

We insert these stories here to reaffirm Cloward and Ohlin's notion that its not always easy to be delinquent or to have delinquent gang formation. Civilized society cannot of course condone a type of repressive activities that will keep gangs out. This is where the functions of policing often come in conflict: to be re-active or pro-active; to protect the commonweal or promote the general welfare.

It is interesting to note about gangs that Cloward and Ohlin developed a typology of delinquent gangs: Criminal type; Conflict type; and Retreatist type. (*ibid.* 20-27) These latter two were also called, respectively, "bopper" and "cat." The latter, the "cat" gang, centered its activities around drugs. After positing three types, they proceed to concern themselves only with the middle or violent gang. We suggest that there is only one type. Indeed others like Yablonsky (*op.cit.*) have pointed to delinquent gangs having an extremely varied agenda of illegal/illicit activities.

But we are uncomfortable with the development of any typology. These often orderly listings (taxonomies) of gangs never seem to catch reality. The "Criminal type" of Cloward and Ohlin for instance, is really a *non sequitur*; all sorts of officials in corrections -- police, probation and parole, institutional staff and more -- *intuit* that the way to describe a delinquent gang is opposite conventional notions of criminality. Adolescent behavior does not have the rational, reasonableness about it. It is with a great deal of skepticism that we give any credit to media stories of juvenile involvement in predatory activities that make sense from an adult standpoint. We do read of juveniles becoming involved on the fringes of organized crime, especially running in drugs and decoying in other ventures. Usually stories such as these, when investigated to the fullest, will reveal that the juveniles have been used by adult crime groups and individuals. The juveniles are not part of the predatory operation any more than the computer itself is a part of embezzlement.

When Louis Yablonsky wrote about the violent gang, one of his insights was to call it a "near group." Even as before, in chapter three we spoke of the delinquent role as having a "flickering" quality to it, a fragility from which one could only infer a kind of temporary and transitory existence, so also does the delinquent gang appear. The gang is not an army platoon; it is not an office department. Its existence is temporary, fragile, on-again-off-again. This does not mean that during brief periods it is docile. Quite the opposite. While it is a (violent) delinquent gang it can be quite dangerous.

Yablonsky also noted the make-up of the violent gang: the inner core of near psycho-paths and all the rest, the marginals. Our own observations of delinquent gangs were in institutional settings. One becomes aware that there are different social relations within a gang. It is doubtful that gangs can ever be truly investigated. They can be dangerous. When they are not dangerous, investigations as to their nature can sometimes lead to the conclusion that the researcher is being taken. Even Yablonsky wondered about this point. Was the particular group (gang) using him? There has been biographical work on delinquent gangs in the past. Although not particularly illuminating on ganging activities, the *Jack Roller* of Clifford Shaw, and the follow up work on the *Jack Roller at Seventy* by Snodegrass gives some interesting insights into the biographical. Our impression is that biographical studies can be overly self serving. Can any be remembered where the protagonist is portrayed as uninteresting?

Again, we think that there are significant social relationships within the delinquent gang. A few develop into social roles. In detention, gangs always seemed to have the leader, perhaps another second or even a third leader. There was always an ordered arrangement. Gangs are not democratic. Most interesting to us was the role of another type within the gang. Either the role was not always played out in detention, or perhaps for some reason, it was not always evident; but from time to time we became aware of a kind of especially violent juvenile gang member. He seemed to be enforcing gang goals, or what? Our interest in institutional tranquility was that if there was such a person, we identify and isolate him.

Perhaps it is in the literary world that we best see a picture of the gang, although it is not of the juvenile delinquent gang. Mario Puza and his work on the *Godfather* is fascinating. Equally well done is Truman Capote's *Glass House*. Although it would be foolhardy to apply the descriptions of adult gangs made by these two authors directly to juvenile gangs, some provocative questions are raised concerning the playing out of roles in groups. How, for instance, are gang leadership roles maintained through the violence of another gang member? How also, does institutional staff condescension become reciprocal to inmate ingratiation and cynicism? Certainly these and other social interactions within confinement institutions were quite perceptively described by both Puza and Capote.

One of the more venerable explanations of human behavior with both longevity and general acceptance is that of role theory.(Znaniecki 1952; Mackey, Miller,and Fredericks 1989) Sometimes this goes under the name of interactionist theory. In that period following the first World War and on through the 1950's, some very prestigious sociologists were calling for role studies of many of societal dimensions.[4]

Anomy theory, although sometimes thought of as standing on its own, is really a part of role or interactionist theory. Anomy is a concept that denotes normlessness, as any freshman introductory student will tell you. But it has better definitions. It connotes that people are not behaving as they say they do. It is really a disparity, a disagreement, a discontinuity between precept and practice--between what people *say* they do and what they really do. It is surprising that there has not been more reported in the correctional literature on institutional investigations of anomy. Earlier work by Srole (1956), McClosky and Schaar (1965) and others on such variables as politics, religion, and student attitudes/ achievement as they related to anomy seemed promising. Whether anomy as a variable was more psycho-social in nature than it was a measure of group normlessness was taken up by Srole. He even introduced the concept of *eunomia* (individual normlessness) to distinguish from the concept of *anomy*, which he held more pertained to a general normlessness of the group--communities for the most part. This distinction has not met with widespread acceptance within the sociological literature. In any event, not much has been done here. (Anomy is sometimes written as *anomie*, or as *anomia* which is the early French or earlier Latin spellings; *anomique* is the adjective form of the word.)

It would seem that correctional institutions would be excellent places for an understanding of this concept of anomy as it applies to whole communities of incarcerated people. A strong case could be made that it could easily be turned into an indicator of institutional viability--whether or not the institution was workable, whether or not the institution was about to "come apart at the seams."

And it has been made quantifiable with paper/pencil questionnaires. But then again, nothing in the correctional literature reflects an interest here. Too bad. Much too much reliance for institutional viability has been placed on the recidivism variable, and as noted elsewhere this can be and is manipulated by vested interests.

But if anomy "theory" has been neglected as a part of role theory, other aspects have not. It was back in 1961 that the Provo Experiment, as it was called, was put into place in Utah. (Empey and Erickson 1972) It was a direct attempt to apply sociological principles of role theory to practice. In a closed setting, "chosen" delinquents were put in interaction with their peers; only a minimal amount of staff intrusion was supposed to occur. The boys were in the closed situation only during discussion periods; in other words they were inmates only during daytime hours, returning to home and community after the group sessions. The main point of the interaction was to apply group norms, to exert pressures for conformity from the group.

Closely related to the Provo Experiment are other action and intervention programs like that at the Redwing Reformatory in Minnesota. There the program went under the name of PPC: Positive Peer Culture. (Vorrath and Brendtro 1974) But the similarities of the two are evident. There has been mixed review of success of these types of programs. Critics often point out that the participants "see through" the often game like atmosphere, and that there is very little carry-over into life after release from the programs.

Critics also insist that the institutions embarking on these programs only want institutional goals met, that is, to keep order, harmony, and no violence. We think this last criticism is undeserved; anyone who has worked in a confinement institution knows, *really knows* that the institutional goal of holding down at least, and/or eliminating mayhem and violence at best is a worthwhile goal, both in and by itself. And we would also urge more and better monitoring of programs which use peer pressures to try to reform. We suspect that what goes on as reported failure may be traceable to too little monitoring. Interestingly, those that started the Provo Experiment indicated a basic truth of human interaction: we all know, suspect or have this "gut knowledge" when the interaction is a sham. Several writers have addressed this. (see especially Matza; Yablonsky)

Again along the path of role theory, although much narrowed, has been an interest in the concept of self esteem as it relates to delinquency. Although there is much to be impressed about here, it would seem that there are so many studies that focus on such narrow goals. Perhaps this will result in better understandings in the long haul, but we are impatient. A recent study on self-esteem and its reciprocal relationship to delinquency is impressive. (Rosenberg, Schooler, and Schoenbach 1989). The researchers not only discover the class link/delinquency to self esteem; they point out the self esteem generating capacity of delinquency itself. (Although a sarcastic critic might say we knew that before, . . .but now we "really" know it.)

There are a few more explanations of behavior as related to delinquency that we wish to address here. Over the past several decades there has been an increasing reliance on what is called the *medical model*. An understanding of this model is that the premises, concepts, the ideas, the whole language of medicine is taken over and by analogy, applied to social science problems. For our interests this would be an application to the problem of delinquency. So then we find that the concepts of disease and health, sickness and wellness, recovery, and even rehabilitation, cancer, infirmity and so forth being applied to delinquent behavior. This is not new. And we expect that the usage will grow.

A little over a decade ago another social problem was truly thought to be a function of social interaction. We have recently asked students how many believe that alcoholism is biologically inherited? All of the students believe that it is; such is the weight of societal agreements. They also classify it as a sickness. We do not want to argue over this social problem. We merely wish to point out how the etiology of alcoholism has moved in the direction of being covered under the umbrella of the medical model.

This same phenomena is occurring for the social problems of delinquency and crime. A few years ago Wilson and Heernstein (1985) reported on an impressive study of deviant behavior (crime). Their conclusion: biological inheritance! We've heard this before of course, but we almost wonder when/if the same scene will be re-enacted for the problem of delinquency. Perhaps not. But a student perusing the correctional literature cannot help but be impressed (shocked) by the call for medical intervention. The notes on connecting biological heredity to delinquency are far more pervasive than in the past.

In 1971 President Richard Nixon's personal physician publicly suggested a nation wide screening for all six year old (boys) for evidence of the XYY chromosome deficiency. He would have identified youngsters for therapeutic intervention at that early age. (Thornton *et al* 1987: 95-96) Good grief!! Though there is a statistical connection of the chromosome deficiency to crime--notably its observed presence in prison populations--we really don't know why the connection exists. But if a person wanted to look for strange statistical correlations in the behavioral sciences he would not go away empty handed.

A few years back we were at one of the conferences on criminal and juvenile justice in Wisconsin. Quite a few of the speakers kept referring to the medical model. It seemed to the writers of this monograph "as if" there was just too much reference given to this model, paradigm, theoretical base or whatever. Since a few of the speakers were interested in cross-cultural comparisons, we could not help but observe that, whereas in American society the criminal justice people opt for explanations *via* the medical model, in Soviet society it appears to be the reverse. Medical people there opt for explanations *via* the criminal justice model! (There is a criminal justice model: we just don't hear much about it as such). Since the conference (1985), we note that no less a sociologist than the late Talcott Parsons (1958) made a similar, *albeit* oblique reference to Soviet medicine as compared to the *United States*. He stated that illness is more of a threat to achievement in the U.S.; whereas it is a threat to responsibility in Russia. Therefore, in the Soviet, illness becomes "suspect;" psychoanalysis in particular is seen as a threat to Soviet value structure since it places greater stress on individual non-responsibility. We're not sure how far one can go in this cross-cultural note on the use of different explanatory models, but it is interesting. It deserves a doctoral dissertation. It also probably points out the transitory nature of theory building and ascendancy, together with the kind of political messages that lie in the background.

On *Violent Crime*: As noted elsewhere, there has been a remarkable change in American Juvenile Justice over the past four-plus decades. One of these changes has been to call violent behavior by juveniles "crime." Not that changing the name impacts on the kind of behavior addressed among either the juveniles or the practitioners. There is, however, general consensus that violent behavior has been on the increase in recent years; this seems obvious not only for juveniles but also for adult deviant behavior. Violent crime still reflects the behavior of a relatively small population of delinquents; this is noted on comparisons for all types of delinquency referral. The reason for the arousal of interest in violent crime then is its *relative* increase. But also there appears a consensus among practitioners that the violent acts in and by themselves appear different, generally, from the past. Adjectives like cruel, vicious, unspeakable, depraved, and the like seem more common today. In the earlier years of juvenile justice, during that period before the "just deserts" agenda, the definition of the concept of crime precluded juveniles. The use of the term *crime* was not acceptable around Juvenile Courts.

Yablonsky offers a vivid descriptive outlook on the violent delinquent gang in which he paints the picture of inner core youth that formerly would best be described as psychopathic or sociopathic. We know it is not in vogue to use these words; but feel that as long as they are used to describe rather than explain, it is reasonable.

There have been numerous attempts to explain violent crime. Focus on the "bad seed" (atavistic, biogenesis), or on the "madness of two" (*folie a deux*), or on the "copycat" violence, or the ghostly double, *der Doppelganger* effect (Bennis 1973) have all been intriguing. Probably not overly useful, but never-the-less intriguing.

We would like to focus on only one concerted attempt to understand violent crime, and we will do this with two quotations:

We venture to claim that (these) investigators have established the existence of aggressive offenders and have demonstrated that *parental rejection* is a factor of major importance in this behavior. ...In short, scientific candor compels us to conclude that the link between *parental rejection** and *aggressive conduct* is one of the more *firmly* established generalizations concerning delinquency. (Gibbons 1986: 191)

Set in context, but opposing this strong view and statement, we find:

> ...despite a number of studies and testimonials which *infer* that various forms of maltreatment increase the probability of violence and like behavior among the victims of such abuse, ...much of the research is methodologically unsound. Any definitive statements alleging a maltreatment-delinquency link are wholly conjectural at this time. ...research indicates that *neglect* has *less impact* on the commission of violent offenses than overt physical abuse of a child, but that *neglect* correlates highly with the commission of property offenses. (Thornton *et al* 1982: 207) (*italics* added)

So where does this leave us? The statements above are diametrically opposed. And they are typical of those found in the literature. To quote Tevya from *Fiddler on the Roof* when he was asked where tradition started, ..."I will tell you, ...I don't know."

Gut level intuiting, and we are inclined to agree with Gibbon's observations and assessment. However, maybe we're appealing more to common sense than to scientific candor. Reason and ration indicates to us a plausible and negative relation between parental rejection of any sort and subsequent deviant behavior--of any sort.

Single factor explanations of delinquency: Gordon Allport (Lindzey 1954: Chap.I) writes about the "simple and sovereign" theories that had enjoyed a long history as basic explanatory models of behavior. After noting eight such theories, models, paradigms or whatever (Hedonism, Cynicism, Altruism, etc., etc.) he goes on to discredit their use. But even noting their singularly "simple and sovereign" quality confers upon them a kind of pejorative status. We are already inclined not to accept them as models.

So it is with all of those explanations of human behavior, in our case the social problem of delinquency. There have been and continue to be, attempts to unlock the mystery; so much concern for the one single factor that will somehow explain it all. All that needs be done is to search; eventually it will or must be found. We would liken this to a kind of **scientific alchemy**.

Where the Alchemist of folklore was trying, ever trying to change base metal (usually lead) into gold, his modern social scientific counterpart tries to find the one key variable that will explain it all.

So the list of single factor explanations of delinquency goes on and it is long: television, comic books, religion, the auto, the working mother, poverty, affluence, ... and on and on. There is nothing wrong with a consideration of these factors; indeed a competent social history of a delinquency would be lacking without these descriptive pieces of information. Our quibble with the single factor theories, and we are not alone, is that they are over-simplistic descriptive pictures.

One of the most overworked single factor theories has been the focus on The Family as it relates to delinquency. Again we caution here; we cannot turn our backs on this important social institution. However, most all that we have seen in consideration of the family impact on deviant behavior is descriptive. Whether it is of the broken home, the middle or lower class, the absent father, the working mother, the intergenerational welfare chain,...it is all descriptive. Where delinquency connections and observations are made, we find too many exceptions for credibility.

And yet among the practitioners, among the experts in the correctional field, if you listen to them in private you will continue to hear the drum-beat: The family did it! The family is responsible.

A story is *apropos* at this time. We once observed a very young, obviously dependent child before a Juvenile Court Judge. The hearts of all those watching went out in sympathy. The judge then wanted to have the parent(s) brought in! The social workers testimony: "they're deceased your Honor." Then the judge called for the grandparents or whoever was responsible for the child. "They're all deceased, your Honor." The judge then asked *who* was responsible for the child. "No one is, your Honor. The child is homeless." The judge seemed deflated. It would not have gone well in that courtroom that day for those responsible for that child, ...that is, if any could be found.

One time we spoke to a prosecutor in Chicago about blaming parents for delinquency. This is a perennial activity of the Press and the ubiquitous public. Sometimes it makes sense; often it does not. The prosecutor tried to educate us on the law in our Western, civilized nation; that at the root of the legal problem of holding parents responsible was the Common principle that, in Law, the parent is NOT responsible, etc., etc. When we persisted he gave us a little poem that is not forgotten:

> Big fleas have little fleas,
> that on their backs do bite them.
> And little fleas have much little'r fleas,
> that do also, ...*ad finitem.*

What was meant to be instructed was the dead-end task of affixing responsibility either in respect to parental responsibility before the law, or as we further interpret, attempting to impute too much to the complexity of the relationship of the family to the social problem of delinquency. For anyone who has perused a family case history, where *several generations* of family members were written about, with the common social problems of the times, the above poem becomes quite instructive. Just where, at what point, can "blame" be affixed? Where can it be pointed out that it all started? Our advice is not to attempt to try.

One other concern we have in this chapter goes not so much to explanatory models or hypotheses of delinquency or how authorities have reacted to control that growing problem in the United States; but to a broader theory of government usually addressed by the political scientists. One implication that reasonably flows from an explanation of the democratic ideal is to invoke what is referred to as the *principle* of *subsidiarity.* Cronin (1959) has pointed to the extremes of governmental intervention and control or withdrawal from the exercising of control when he noted that:

> Statism, for example, is evil because it seeks to enhance the power of the state as such, even to the point of denying essential rights of citizens. Socialism is wrong because it emphasizes the material element in society, to the exclusion of more important values. An over-centralized state arrogates to itself functions that can and will be performed properly by lower bodies. This violates the principle of subsidiarity, which holds that 'power and responsibility should be decentralized as far as the general welfare permits.'
>
> (Cronin 1959: 75)

When we earlier addressed the conflict between conservatives and their new liberal friends against the older liberals, the dimensions of the controversy were seen as emphasizing the just deserts/minimal intrusion into the lives of individuals for deviant transgressions, OR emphasizing benevolent intervention/rehabilitation. It seems to us that much of the controversy was over which point on the continuum --the individual to collective --ought be the point where intervening was most appropriate. Assuming that all of the parties concerned with delinquency problems and solutions possess good will, and we do assume this, then much of the argument over interventions, incapacitation, rehabilitation, AND de-institutionalization, de-criminalization is over who or what unit ought have the responsibility to do something about the problem, and when.

It has been our thinking that the strong individualism so much written about in the U.S. has emphasized the subsidiarity principle as stated above. We have no quarrel with this principle; indeed we believe that the "sticky" point in its definition is agreement over what constitutes the "common good." But we also believe men of good will can come to some agreement through dialogue and compromise.

We would prefer to restate the principle of subsidiarity as follows: power and responsibility should be *centralized* only as far as the general welfare permits. This does not substantially change the definition; it does reverse the direction as to deciding who should handle social problems. Are there problems for the individual, the family, the neighborhood, the community, . . . the STATE? When considering the common good, our society in the past emphasized individualism. Without sacrificing individual freedoms we can approach problem solutions by looking to group and communal action where and when it is most appropriate.

We argue here that the state does have an interest and obligation to care for those affected by serious social problems inherent in any system of competing relations. Emphasizing a higher order of responsibility, from individual to the State, places the onus for action where it belongs: where the power exists.

Later, we would like to return to this consideration. In addressing the many problems in delinquency, crime, and deviance of all sorts, it appears most obvious to us that, while we must start with the individual, we must look to family, to neighbor, and to an ever widening rendering of community. That the individual is powerless in much of our modern urban world has been a theme of many writers, not only in the erudite social sciences, but also in the contemporary mass media and the "best seller" literature. Responsibility as well as power to affect change ought be,... no must be... commensurate. Power and responsibility should go hand in glove.

Chaos Theory, Delinquency, and the Plot:
All of the behavioral science explanations of human activity can be classified as resting on the Newtonian thesis of an ordered universe. In this sense the ordered world is *linear*; all that occurs is ultimately predictable as with the precision and ingenuity of the master clockmaker. Isaac Newton,

with his mathematical calculus of the universe, had given the Faith to Science, the faith that all was knowable if only we could gather enough data. Even for Newton, though, certain "quirks" in nature required a Prime Mover to press the "reset" button every once in a while. Sir Isaac died in 1727. (Taylor 1989)

This faith was ultimately eroded in the nineteenth century; predictability based on more and more--ever more--information was sorely tested, particularly by way of the development of statistical mechanics, the study of gaseous motion. Scientists from this particular discipline had concluded that complexity--real complexity--led to uncertainty. In essence, the thesis was introduced that small forces *can* and *do* have an effect all out of proportion; disproportionate interaction is thus *chaotic*, or *non-linear*. Whereas Newtonian thinking is linear, the essence of chaos is that the thinking is non-linear.

Another contemporary theorist (a Climatologist), Edward Lorenz has introduced the concept of the "butterfly effect" to portray the vast multitude of actions that occur and would have to be accounted for in prediction based on linearity. (Taylor *op.cit.*) The conclusion: this is not theoretically possible. It becomes especially impossible because non-linear (chaotic reasoning) has established that action has a peculiar sensitivity to initial conditions; there is a magnification of the consequences.

All of this would be particularly discouraging if it were not for some recent work in Cardiology. According to Taylor, no respectable cardiological team is complete without its resident non-linear dynamicist. Fibrillation is evidence of chaos in heart attack patients. Specialists have been perplexed as to how to handle it. They have been encouraged recently by focusing on *how* fibrillation occurs, rather than *why*.

Essentially, the non-linear focus is on the structures of randomization. The conclusion is that natural systems follow *similar routes* in the transition from order to chaos. So, the exciting news is that patterns can be discerned in what for all intent and appearance is random!

An example of patterns in randomization is the *thinking process*. The concepts of *optimization of solution* and *constrained random* refer to the processes whereby the thinking individual sorts out the desirable from the undesirable conclusion. The thought search, while appearing random, in reality is quite selective for its target. We suppose that everyone has had this kind of experience; many memories and ideas are "whisked over" until the desired one is "locked in." If the process of random thinking were truly random,...one conclusion would be as "good" and desirable as any other,...but such is not the case. The *normal* EEG patterning is chaotic and turbulent; the *non-normal EEG* pattern is quite orderly, as in the case of epileptic seizure.

So the good news is that while dynamic complexity and sensitivity to initial conditions militates against order and pattern, ...predictability is still possible through searching out the variations of non-predictability. Such is the focus of chaos theory or non-linearity.

What does all of this hold for the behavioral sciences, and for the study of delinquency in particular? Currently there are two broad theoretical stances in sociology: *order* and *conflict*. We submit that these two both subscribe to linear thinking. The conflict theorists are *not* non-linear, as might be suggested by the term *"conflict"*. Some time ago Robert K. Merton (1961) taught that research in the social sciences ought not so much focus on the *why* of behavior, but rather to focus on the *"how does it work"* part of the equation. Perhaps he was really on to something.

We have always been uncomfortable with some of the conclusions and implications in delinquency research. Undoubtedly a great deal of faith was placed in the linear axiom of random order. Thus, the inferences that delinquency cuts across the social classes and ethnic lines, or that we are all"...but for the Grace of God," delinquent, never have set well. Political expediency notwithstanding, the ring of accuracy appears absent. We have taught elsewhere that delinquency is better described through *normative dispersion* rather than random scatter, as the above would imply. This suggests that there are *patterns*, and that they are normative.[5]

Currently, there is nothing in the delinquency literature that addresses non-linearity, chaos thinking. We suggest that attention may be overdue. Not only could the emphases of study be on delinquent acts within communities, but also the individual delinquent. Thus, the patterning of behavior, however random or by chance it may appear, could be focused upon. Chaos theory additionally has introduced the concepts of *"sensitivity to initial conditions"* and *"magnification of consequences"* that ought be addressed by the behavioral sciences. That they have not as yet is probably more a reflection on the fact that linearity and order theory has no competent way of using them.

In the next chapter, we intend to write about the audience to delinquency in a modern urban world. And in chapter six we want to address urbanism and urbanization as two reciprocal themes that account for much of our contemporary problems of delinquency. To this extent we will want to pay attention to some of the earlier writers on the nature of city living for people -- for mankind.

The beginning of the twentieth century witnessed two schools of thought in sociology with respect to "the city," the German school and the Chicago school. In much of the earlier work that was representative of the thinking of these two schools, one idea appears evident. This was the theme that the city, with its evolving social and spatial forms, offered to mankind the ability to be free from the constraints of nature. This was most often called individuation; to be morally and intellectually free. The two schools differed somewhat on what that freedom entailed; but never-the-less, both schools essentially agreed that a kind of evolutionary process occurred in the history of the city whereby man's spirit was opened. From the German school we see that Spengler observed that:

> ... man as civilized, as intellectual nomad, is again wholly microcosmic, wholly homeless, as free intellectually as hunter and herdsman were free sensually. (Sennett 1969: 65)

And from the Chicago school, Robert Park suggests that:

> social changes . . .have their inception in events which 'release' the individuals out of which society is composed. Inevitably, however this release(d) (*sic*) is followed in the course of time by the reintegration of the individuals so released into a new social order. In the meantime, however, certain changes take place--at any rate they are likely to take place -- in the character of the individuals themselves. They become, in the process, not merely emancipated, but enlightened. The emancipated individual invariably becomes in a certain sense and to a certain degree a cosmopolitan.
>
> (Sennett *op.cit.* p.137)

And again, although referring to the development of a city-based *bourgoisie* of craftsmen, artisans and merchants, Palen notes (1987: 43) that there was a German phrase that expressed not only the spirit of that time, a break with the manorial, feudal systems, but also expressed the spirit of city life: *Stadtluft macht frei!*, or "City air makes free!"[6]

As we have earlier suggested the development and implementation of unions for correctional workers, and as we recommended that children be educated and socialized in the manners and morals of city living, we have done so with an eye toward recognition of the historical and philosophical purposes of urbanism and urbanization. Indeed, a number of urbanologists have suggested that individual persons, acting alone, cannot reach the kind of goals and purposes that can be accomplished collectively. In a modern, urban, and democratic society, political action is best obtained through associations, not individual efforts.   Perhaps the best known of advocates for collective action in recent years was the late Sol Alinsky. His efforts and organizational skills resulted in more than one solution of intractable social problems. Poplin (1979: 256-57) has called Alinsky's method the "Power Bloc" approach, noting that no other name is so closely associated with the radical perspective of community development.[7]

If the broad purpose, the value of city living is to be free, then city dwellers, citizens, must come to terms with what is entailed.   Cities are not natural to mankind, except in the sense that they are men's creation. And city living for mankind is a relatively short period in his history. Of the hundreds of thousands of years he has been on this earth, only in a few recent thousand has he been urbanized -- civilized. We think that delinquency, as well as all of the other social problems involving roles we play statuses we occupy, are traceable to a lack of coping with that which is city-like, not only as "ways of life," but also as processes of becoming a city, of citification, of urbanization.

We do not believe that children are born to intuitively or instinctively come to terms with city living. Urbanism is a way of life, as Wirth so aptly expressed. But delinquency is a fractured expression of that way of life. We know that this is another way of saying that it is norm violations.   It is different however in its emphasis on inarticulate means of expression of community interests.

ENDNOTES FOR CHAPTER FOUR

1. We are indebted to Professor Stuart McIlraith, a Zoologist, for this analogical story. While it may be overly facetious as critical of behavioral research and theory, it does get a point across.

2. Transactional analysis seems to have faded into the back-ground as far as a technique for handling offenders. During the nineteen-seventies it was the up-and-coming strategy. *Time* magazine had called it a kind of "pop psychoanalysis." Indeed it is easily explained to participants, and young people get caught up in its process, acting as if in a game during analysis.

3. On occasion we have spoken to others about this notion of an optimum time period if detention is to be employed among the techniques of rehabilitation. A time period as short as twenty-four to thirty-six hours appears on the surface to be quite short. This does not disparage the point that *any* incarceration *can* be threatening for the person incarcerated. Still and all it does appear a short time period. One of the court administrators for the LaCrosse Wisconsin Department of Social Services agrees with us on this optimum period. Mr. Pete Dwyer has had extensive experience as a supervising case officer where juveniles were incarcerated for appropriate reasons. This time period of a little more than one day's length appears to be the framework for positive reformative results when juveniles are held.

4. Professor Florian Znaniecki died at the age of seventy-six in nineteen-fifty-eight (1958). He was one of the few most prodigious of American scholars in sociology. His formal academic training was in Philosophy at the University of Crakow, Poland and he is remembered most for his collaboration with Wm. I. Thomas on the life history of the "Polish Peasant in Europe and America." His life was varied and full. He once told his students about his stint with the French Foreign Legion, humorously complaining that he had no veteran's benefits. In 1939 he was Europe bound when word of the Russian military advance into Poland occurred. He returned permanently to the United States, noting that the Russian army under Stalin's direction had massacred some tens-of-thousands of Polish intellectual society at Katyn Forest. He might have been one of those unfortunates. Professor Znaniecki had many of his graduate students direct their attention to the study of social roles. His own study (1940) on the role of the man of knowledge was considered one of the most timely and important monographs of the period.

5. The concept of *random scatter* would appear to be linear to the extent that it derives from an ordered and statistically predictable universe. The concept of *normative dispersion* suggests that there are initial conditions which affect outcomes; and these initial conditions are not apparent as antecedent variables.

6. The original denotation of *Stadtluft macht frei* was that a serf who had fled the indentured service of a landed gentry during the Manoral period of European history could find sanctuary in the burgeoning cities of the time. *If* after a *year* the serf was still free, he would be considered *legally* emancipated. This arrangement had less to do with generosity and charity and had more to do with competition between the landed gentry of the countryside with their city counterparts over a scarce commodity: population. People were still needed as manpower on the manor, but they were equally important for the growth of cities. Cities did not grow from within as they do today; cities were dangerous places to be born and to live. Interestingly, much of modern western city ordinance still has reference to this time period of *one year*. Confinement in city jails was set at no longer a period, while conviction to a felony, a violation of State criminal code, carried with it periods of confinement exceeding this one year limit. Churches and Universities have in more modern times been places of sanctuary for rebels and criminals of the civil order. Though now as then, the honoring of the practice was more in the breech than in the practice.

7. The late Sol Alinsky was as formidable as he was outlandish and outrageous in community organization. A whole methodology has been named after him: the Alinsky method. Basically it was confrontational. There is the story where he one time organized a "sit in" at Chicago's City Hall. Orchestrating several hundred of Chicago's inner city underclass to the site of protest, he first had the busloads' stop for lunch: at a *beanery*! Another person cast in the same mold as Alinsky was the late Professor Gregory Stone of the University of Minnesota. We had occasion to observe him organize a "take-over" by a large group of the urban underclass at the annual meetings of the Mid-West Sociological Society during the early nineteen-seventies. The meeting was in St. Louis. During the convention dinner banquet, ten minutes before seating, the lights went out. Dr. Stone had personally pulled the switch. When the lights went on, all the tables were occupied by St. Louis resident indigents. Sometimes these tactics worked better than others. This time in St. Louis the targeted population were mostly from the discipline of sociology, where liberal credentials are not in short supply. Dr. Stone seemed most unhappy that there was no indignation or protest registered.

5
The Audience

Of all those involved in the equation of the juvenile delinquency problem, it is the omnipresent public that will stand to lose the most. Whether submissively resigned as victim, as is so often the case for our elderly population, or actively engaged as a catalyst for change in the form of juvenile justice practitioner, there is a significant cost for the participants. The sequels of the many delinquency scripts have a high price. The audience will pay directly or indirectly; actively and directly in terms of individual hurt and/or destroyed lives and property; passively and indirectly through lost social and material community wealth and well being.

It is quite often difficult to figure out what the general public wants or expects from its problem solvers, both the public servants and the private sector persons. This thought is not new. Those responsible for public policy and its implementation have complained for years that they receive mixed messages: solve the social problem of errant youth; be careful of civil liberties while doing so. Have more places to care for our deviant populations and social problem cases; disengage, decriminalize, and deinstitutionalize. Hire more police; cut the budget and the taxes. One would have to wonder how so many mixed and seemingly incompatible messages can be delivered simultaneously.

Perhaps the real problem here is a failure to understand the difference between control and prevention. Sociologists have long understood the basic differences between these two concepts. The former (control) connotes an intervention only after the fact of deviance, while the latter (prevention) means exactly that which is stated, ...preventing deviance from occurring in the

103

first place.   A serious fault involved in understanding prevention is the question of verification.   How does one show that delinquency was prevented from happening?   For programs where the goal is *not* so much to reform deviants, but rather to prevent occurrence,... where is the empirical evidence that it works?

It might have been better to have called the prevention programs --where they existed at all-- curtailment ventures.   In this way we might not have anticipated too much.   The general public, though, has come to anticipate, to expect success stories for their tax dollars.   The social scientists, the policy implementers, the press people, and all of the "experts" and those privy to insider knowledge should have educated the masses in this regard. Perhaps it is in the context of an "oversell" to the people that experts have been responsible for presenting a cultural imperative that expects too much. This has been in many fields and disciplines; note for instance medicine, general education, and environmental problems, to name a few.

We think that one of the sources of an "oversell" of success expectations to the public has been the gradual implanting of a "business model" within much of our culture.   How often are the "...can do!," or "...when the going gets tough, ...the tough get going!" or "...do it, damn it!" slogans heard in everyday life?   As fodder for commerce and public relations, heraldic insignias may be just dandy; for real life social and inter and intra-group relations they are a farce.

Messages from the public in the form of editorials, letters to the editor, social critic columns, mass media reports, and general dialogue and talk shows, all have their political philosophy and agenda that readily becomes apparent.   For the conservative, the driving force behind the concern for civil liberties and solicitude has been one of *nobless oblige,* a commitment to the social contract;   for the liberal, that force has been one of heartfelt compassion.   We will have to leave it to future generations to verify which of the two is more stable and more reliable.

We have previously addressed the argument of conservatives and liberals over agenda and implementation by earlier generations of practitioners in corrections. That argument is equally apparent for the general public today.   Now, however, only the basic philosophical leanings are discernable.   Either "get tough" and crack down on the recalcitrants, delinquents, and deviants, or, ..."have a heart" and remember our children, our culture, and our future.   And yet these ideologies and values are extremely important.   They simply cannot be summarily dismissed or implemented in a cavalier manner.   For the most part they chart the paths of the future for any direction of delinquency control or curtailment.

Many, many authors have asserted that in terms of the problem of delinquency, a society gets what it asks for. This is a sort of variation of the old functionalist viewpoint, that somehow, the problem is part of the solution of social system (society) viability. Even those who do not buy this reasoning also point out the obverse or reciprocal, that the individual delinquent gets that which is asked for: the powerless interacting with the powerful. For the general public though, the idea that society is part of the problem of delinquency (or for that matter any social problem) is repugnant. People don't like it. Liberals in particular, but perhaps the social scientists in general, have taken much criticism for suggesting it. Critical commentary would assert that it would be unreasonable at best and irrational at worst to conclude that society would somehow want to have a social problem. The thinking is that since a reasonable, responsible person would not choose a problem for himself, neither would a whole society.

But what of the general public's acceptance of delinquency in the community? Does society really get what it asks for? It seems to be quite common sense that everyone is against the problem. As a society though, we are quite tolerant of individual variation and deviation. That this is the case can be seen as the source of much that is good in our American democratic system. It would go beyond the purposes of this monograph to argue this point further. Somehow it appears that the public "knows" when the boundaries of social action have been stretched to the point where "so called" innocent peccadillos become not so innocent delinquencies.

That we are willing to blur the distinction between delinquency and non delinquency, crime and the criminal, alcoholism and sobriety, and many other forms of social problem people can be seen in our everyday use of the word "alleged." Witness TV news reports, weekly news journals, and all other means of mass communication. Even where it is abundantly clear and openly obvious, the imputation of allegation only is attached. While we can certainly understand the legal implications and judicial niceties involved here, what purpose is served outside of the adjudicatory process and the courtroom itself? We have known street-wise juvenile delinquents who laughingly referred to their own deviant conduct as "alleged." The street language adds humor that clearly debauches meaning.

A further comment on our societal willingness to accept quite a bit of deviation from acceptable behavior is seen in the following story that we believe is part of our cultural heritage. We had occasion to observe a television newscast one time when the then President of the United States was awarding the Medal of Honor to a young soldier. The year was 1967 and the President was Lyndon Johnson. The young soldier's father was standing, very proudly, next to his son. President Johnson asked the young man about his future plans. Before he could answer, the father gushed with both enthusiasm and satisfaction "...its a mighty poor country that can't afford a son to bum around for awhile." President Johnson was noticeably perturbed. He had missed the point. The father was paraphrasing an old Celtic (Irish) adage. ("It's a mighty poor family that can't afford a lady or a gentleman.") The meaning behind this is that there is an acceptance of some lifestyles of deviation. Our history and our culture converge to bring meaning in the present.

John Steinbeck (1972), Erskine Caldwell (1940), and Margaret Mitchell (1966) observed the Celtic culture as a part of our rural Southern heritage. It was authors such as these that have most contributed to a kind of Southern mystique.[1] Indeed, one hypothesis on the cause of our Civil War has it that the conflagration was in reality the acting out of an age old rivalry between the Celtics of Ireland and Scotland, pitted against the Angles and Saxons, mostly from England, but all from the isles of Britain. The former (Celts) with their laid back culture were once again involved in murderous conflict with the industrious and pedantic WASP's. Though interesting, it is hypothetical.

Our purpose in pointing this out is really two-fold. *One,* cultural traditions are still operative in the U.S. that have their beginnings in a long history, some of which value a tradition of deviance; and *two,* as indicated earlier in our second chapter, ...successful communication of such values and ideas are at best quite tenuous. The messages become garbled in the larger national society over time.

Concerning cultural traditions and deviance, it is surprising that not much attention has been devoted in the study of delinquency to this topic. In presentations of crime, this subject has been presented, more so in literary work than in the social sciences. Puzo's work (1969) in particular, emphasizing the Italian connection is obvious. Field workers in juvenile corrections cannot help but notice the generational and ethnic impact, with accompanying traditions, that show up as delinquent patterns.

Although the conclusions are quite impressionistic that certain "types" or groups are more involved in delinquent lifestyles than others, there does seem to be a kind of consensus among correctional practitioners that the "hillbillies" (Mountain Williams' as they would describe themselves) are a source of delinquency. Likewise, the "Gypsies" are another group that come to the attention of authorities. While we understand that these are pejorative labels and are quite stigmatizing, our interest here is in pointing out the long histories of cultural traditions that are operative in urban life. And these traditions began elsewhere. Many of these groups that find themselves in the large U.S. Metropolitan areas are constantly moving. School officials particularly are perplexed at the record keeping involved in multiple transfers among schools and districts. There are some of these extended family systems that even resent their children attending school, opting to train them in small time petty burglary and theft.

Of a greater interest in cultural traditions as they relate to delinquency would be those values that were passed on, generation to generation, with respect to ethnic, religious, and social class backgrounds. To be sure Walter Miller (1958) has documented his observations on the lower class family and delinquency, and by extension of his reasoning, to the middle class. But it is our contention that values like Miller's "focal concerns" as they relate to delinquency have shallow roots. Except perhaps, for the tradition of survival, the other imperatives to delinquency that are often cited as being of lower class origin (trouble, toughness, macho, excitement, fatalism, etc.) would more properly be *situational*, and not passed on except within the delinquent subculture: the gang itself. To be sure, while studying delinquent gang behavior and supposed related values, Miller might well be accused of developing a tautology: were the values emanating from the home to the street *or* from the street to the home? It would not be the last time that circular reasoning had permeated studies of social class behavior.

We note, for instance, that in Jewish cultural tradition, while the *Talmud* ascribes to kindness, peace, love, charity, and compassion, all of which are virtues shared with both Islam and Christianity, *survival* (*self preservation*) is placed ahead of these (Greenberger:1991). For Judaism, survival is *number one*. This in no way is a condemnation. Certainly other ethnics, religious and cultural groups have traditions that are handed down. We would like to see a greater emphasis in a sociology that draws attention to the consequences of these for delinquency patterns.

The messages that come to and from the public (our audience) are filtered through the ubiquitous mass media; the Fourth Estate; our modern Scribes and Pharisees. We earlier addressed the rule/tradition in delinquency that called for confidentiality. And we "tilted" in favor of openness of information, or at least dialogue on its efficacy. The Press has an awesome task in delivering messages. On the one hand, they must sustain our interest; while on the other, they have no less an obligation to present accurately and truthfully. But that is their chosen assignment. Our Universities are the training ground for this task, and their record so far would probably earn the Press a "gentleman's grade" of "C,"...perhaps the "C+"!! This is not good.

Some time back it was expected that in the late Spring or early Summer, the correctional institutions in particular and the agencies in general would be visited by the newly hired reporters and photographers of the City journals. Apparently their editors didn't quite know what other assignment on which to send them, so they would end up investigating delinquency. The foci of attention were the various institutions and agencies; after all, their locations are fixed and in the "yellow pages." They are easily identified. This was not really investigative reporting as such, but more to the point of getting "human interest" stories. Unfortunately, the results, often published, were mostly sensational journalism. While the general public may have had their interest piqued, objectivity became the victim.

We have in mind one particular occasion where the reporters and photographers ended up taking a picture of a detention facility. In order to have the desired depreciating portrayal the photograph was taken across the street from the facility, but, ...across the street and behind the wrought iron bars of a residential front porch! This had the effect of conveying a truly menacing impression. The photographer could probably have accomplished the same result if a pocket comb was held in front of the camera lens. But where is the objectivity of such reporting?

Public officials, and this would include the bureaucrats in corrections, are generally not at ease with the Press. This is undoubtedly an understatement. It is not only too bad, it is a shame that openness and understanding is not the norm. We do believe that the problem--and it is one of trust--can only be better addressed by training in objectivity and ethical neutrality at the colleges and universities. Not only do prospective journalists need to be trained, but likewise all those entering the so-called professions. Journalists in particular ought be taught to get their stories straight (as one midwest city Judge once remarked in an open meeting); they can still be creative with the language. The real task in human interest stories is to write creatively, ...not to create in writing!

To be sure, messages concerning delinquency do not always come from the Press. Quite another purveyor to the public interest is the mass media as art form. Particularly important are the movies and video portrayals of our modern urban culture. We do not want to address the issue of pornography at length here; but we simply cannot escape the admonition that there is an "awful lot" of meaningless trite that is used to fill in time for the American masses. Whether violence, sex, nudity or other forms of pornography are delinquency related, is not the point. The point is that most of that which our young people are exposed to in the name of entertainment is simply bad taste.

A few decades ago it was the titillating comic books that were the bane of correctional personnel. The cheaply printed and published material couldn't be destroyed fast enough by institutional personnel. Interestingly, most of the destruction of comic book "porno" was a kind of censorship of self defense: conventional wisdom suggested that much criticism would come from parents, officials and other visitors if they happened to notice. Such thinking was not without foundation. Then along came the Biblical comics; stories from the Old Testament put to lurid print and picture. It seems that the American ability to create a profit in business ventures is unrivaled. Pornography had found accomplice in the religious institutions: Chaplains were unsure as to whether material portrayed was or was not to be censored.

When considering a relationship between pornography and delinquency, we would like to observe that there are forms of mass media messages that are not so obviously distasteful as cruelty, violence, nudity and the like. We are particularly concerned with the commercial as a medium of information. Does the reader really know the researched impact of a commercial? Its power is substantial. And what of those commercial messages that urge a hedonism reminiscent of Boccaccio's *Decameron*? Is there a doubt that the messages massage, to paraphrase another popular author? (McLuhan and Fiore:1967)

We had a friend who once won a *Cannes'* best picture award. This was considered quite prestigious among his colleagues. On his own time and with five thousand dollars in personal savings he had put together "The Parable," a truly remarkable film presentation on the Christ, depicted in Circus, as a moral truth. His full time job was creating commercials, ...at seventy five thousand dollars apiece. This was the going rate cost for his commercials, that is. This was over two decades ago and dollar comparisons today would be quite different. But do you doubt that commercials deliver the intended impact? While we know that the purpose is to sell merchandise, we would also worry about that impact, not only for young impressionable minds but also for the adult population who are the significant others for our juveniles, ...the parents, the guardians, the audience in the delinquency equation.[2]

Concerning Victims: Of all those involved as the audience in delinquency scripts it is the large, unorganized masses that are the most affected. They sit "front row center," so to speak. Whether involved directly, having been individually "targeted" in an assault, robbery, burglary or other kind of predatory crime, or indirectly involved as part of a hurt community, they are real. The victims are as the cartoonist of *Pogo* would depict, ...*us. They* is *we!* In a sense we are all victims of crime and delinquency. It is a malaise, a sickness of community.

Specific victims of crime and delinquency are not sure as to how they should act or think about their involvement. When they become part of the process where the correctional apparatus intervenes, either in the court hearing or the follow up period of accounting (either through rehabilitation, incapacitation, or whatever) they do not completely understand the Community's and the State's interests. Matza (1964:169-172) notes that one reason for delinquents' developing the feeling of being "put upon" by the system is that there is a common misunderstanding of the differences between *tort* law and *criminal* law. Tort law allows for the concept of fault; not so with the criminal law. Fault has the corollary of forgiveness. Crime does *not* have this as a deduction from the original proposition. The oblique and dark humor of the police booking sergeant's *leitomotiv* is *apropos*: "To err is human, ...to forgive ...is against departmental policy."

So it is that both victims and perpetrators of delinquent acts commonly misconstrue the nature of the State's response to official delinquency. Most field correctional workers have had that experience where specific victims announce that "...all is forgiven." They have made their peace with the accused. Their surprise that such is *not* the case is a conundrum to all but the supporting cast of the delinquency drama.

An interesting story that supports these observations is taken from the mass media accounting of the Patty Hurst kidnapping of several years ago. It was only after the original headlines detailing the kidnapping appeared that the other story of her complacency in the affair emerged. Immediately after her purported abduction, headlines and media accounts abounded. For all intent and purpose, she had been kidnapped by a group that demanded ransom(s). Her father, William Randolph Hurst, made an emotional public plea to her abductors for her release. Randolph Hurst was not only wealthy, he was heir to a singularly large corporate enterprise of the news media. One would tend to assume that he knew and understood the inherent nature of a crime; how the prosecution of a case would unfold. Yet his public plea for her release by her captors was accompanied by his statement that "... all would be forgiven."

On the heels of his message was an official announcement by the California Prosecutor that indeed, ...all would *not* be forgiven; Patty Hurst's abductors had transgressed Federal statutory law as well as California

Criminal code. The prosecutions office would seek to punish!

So it is not surprising to see victims personalize their relationship with delinquent adversaries. In juvenile courts particularly, victims usually appear satisfied and even exuberant when a finding of delinquency is entered by the judge. Their usual response at that moment is to question when and how they are going to receive compensation. They are non-plused when it is explained to them that civil damages would have to be awarded through other courts. And in the case of delinquent minors, adjudicated delinquents could only become litigants (not defendants) upon reaching their majority. Simply put, victims can sue when their malefactors become legally adult, usually on the twenty first birthday. Needless to say, victims are not pleased with this lesson in civics.

Yet some courts and some judges have attempted to address compensation to victims by violators of the laws. One that has attracted a broad national interest is the activities of Judge Dennis Challeen from Minnesota. Several years back he had started a program where defendants in court were presented with the "opportunity" to do good. Sometimes this doing good was directly aimed at righting a personal redress; the victim was helped "in kind." The defendant was to do something for the victim.

Sometimes the activities were for a public good, like policing the parkways, the shoulders of roads, public areas, and so forth. In back of these good works there was always the threat of incarceration if the adjudicated defendant balked at this type of sentence. Judge Challeen should be commended for his innovativeness. However, he himself is the first to admit that his program is not for every defendant. There are some crimes and some accused that simply do not fit.

Other programs have begun in the recent past. Victim Offender reconciliation has surfaced as a means of trying to reintegrate the offender in the community. (Karmen 1990:291-92; 340-47) Clearly these programs are a form of rehabilitation. The idea of compensation for injury usually takes second place to personal accommodation. The purpose of reconciliation programs is that the face-to-face encounters will accommodate *both* parties of a crime.

While there is nothing wrong with these approaches, we would urge caution. The encounters may make the matter worse. Then too, we are not convinced that non-directed encounters between victims and offenders will lead to positive outcomes all by themselves. There is the tacit understanding of these encounters that an understanding between two people leads inevitably to a satisfactory adjustment (accommodation).   The social science theory upon which this is based is quite superficial.

As Jacob Moreno worked out his conceptualization of role playing as therapy (1961), he clearly had in mind several designs and outcomes. Moreno's *psychodrama* focused on role reversals in an already existing group that comprised two or more status structures; his notion of *sociodrama* was that of playing role reversals where status structures were not significant, but where *collective representations* of reference group norms were played out. From the first (psychodrama) the expectation of personal adjustment was at least plausible; but from the second (sociodrama), the *best* we should expect would be insights into the other persons behavior.

Truly getting along with others and adjusting to their behavior is quite different from knowing why they do what they do.   Victim Offender reconciliation programs need to take into account the potentials.   By this we mean that a great deal of care and thought should be given before implementation.

And as we wrote earlier, the role as a concept of sociology denotes a rather structured entity; even though we view it as quite fragile, it still has considerable resiliency to it. We understand the role of the father, the mother, the policeman, teacher, husband, wife and so forth. Victim Offender relations are only addressing minimal social relations for which there are no role guidelines.   Making up the guideposts to interaction in process can be quite hazardous.

The general public as victim is quite another story. Even when there is an identifiable victim, someone who is hurt, offenders will often speak of the affair as if it were victimless.   The point that the victim may not have been targeted specifically, but just happened to be in the wrong place at the wrong time is often enough for the delinquent/criminal   to conjure the notion of "accident." That there is no intended victim is often enough for young delinquents to personally excuse themselves.   The more so when victims only lose property.   The ones that are seen to be hurt in such a scenario are the large insurance corporations and those businesses and enterprises that are far from everyday life. The community social fabric is not thought important.

Indeed, as a society we have come to that point where much of the real cost of crime and delinquency is "passed on" in the form of higher prices for just about all of life's needs and wants. We know that delinquency, crime, and deviance is there, we just are not capable of realizing the full impact that it has on our way of life. We are shocked at statistical reports detailing millions upon millions of dollars but still turn away because it appears so impersonal.

Some years back the auto insurance industry attempted to make it slightly more difficult to steal a car. Two things seemed most appropriate to set as goals. The introduction of a lock within the steering column so that when the key is not in the ignition the steering wheel would not move has been around for quite a few years. Before this was accomplished, car theft was much easier because after "jumping" the ignition system the auto could be driven. The second thing that the auto insurance industry accomplished, although only superficially, was the introduction of a keying system for the auto ignitions that was slightly better than ludicrous. Years back, it was common knowledge among delinquent youth that many keys were inter- changeable among and between autos. But perhaps the one thing that auto makers and insurance companies can't invent is a way to have drivers remove the keys from the car when it is not in use. Delinquent boys were fond of telling which car would be stolen: "The one with the keys in it!" This still is the *modus opperendi* of auto theft.

It is now more difficult to "jump start" a car without a key because most lock the steering mechanism; difficult but not impossible. A while back all sorts of crude mechanisms of wires, conductors and the like would be employed by delinquents in order to successfully jump an auto. These devices would be recognized as burglary tools and confiscated. We have recollection of a vast array of such crude, homemade devices. One time we remember the appearance of a rather sophisticated jumping apparatus that began to appear on the streets of Chicago's neighborhoods. A fairly large number began to be confiscated by the police. It was like the introduction of a new weapon within the delinquent "turf." Some rather astute police work revealed that the jumper devices were being mass produced at one of the vocational high school's shop classes. Wires were being put together with soldered alligator clips. Very fancy shopwork indeed! Unfortunately the revelation was to the chagrin and dismay of the shop teacher, the principal and the staff of the identified school.

One time at one of the State of Illinois' correctional facilities (at St. Charles, Illinois), a counselor had lost his keys or misplaced them. On a rather blustering winter afternoon a young inmate was called upon, taken to the institution's parking lot, where he jumped the car so that the employee could ride home. This is a particularly revealing insight into the world of delinquency. Counselors themselves quite often know about what is being done, but they can't perform the tasks.

There are other victims besides the general public and particular individuals. To be sure the victims of delinquency are for the most part the delinquents themselves. We do not argue from the standpoint of Conflict or Marxian (Radical) theory which portrays the social system as the perpetrator of aggression, although in other contexts such depictions are not without merit and have reasonable cogency. The purposes of such agendas are blatantly ideological.

Delinquents do prey upon each other. Much of the deviance between and among delinquents has sexual and/or racial undertones. The idea of "booty" refers to a kind of sexual harassment among juveniles. Social scientists did not coin the term; the concept of "booty" comes from the street language. In no way can it be considered play, although the interactionalists (Role theory advocates) among the professionals would call attention to the identities that young males are trying to obtain; maleness and *machismo*.

Practitioners in corrections can and do become victims. They can also be the aggressors. Certainly there is a delicate balance in the human interaction between young delinquents and persons carrying out their jobs. It is easy to spot a novice correctional worker; some "experienced" and "should be" wiser workers never quite adapt. The criticism of a former veteran Sheriff wanting approbation and recommendation from a National Correctional Society was accommodated with the notation that he possessed "...one years experience, repeated twenty times!" Such is the stuff of which careers are ended or severely truncated. He found a new job!

When observing the interaction between a correctional worker and client(s), it is possible to take notice of the assertiveness or intimidation that is taking place. Happily neither will show. Juveniles, particularly unsophisticated to the adult word, will often quite obviously show off their dominance by getting very close physically, sometimes punching their fists into palms, perhaps talking loudly, perhaps thrusting their physical presence and bearing with chin and chest. We've witnessed occasions where young delinquents would "deliberately" trip over the caseworker, step on his shoes, drop some article that he had asked to see, and so forth. When this occurs it is obvious that intimidation has taken over. Most police are trained in assertiveness; caseworkers are not. The balance between assertiveness and intimidation (an active and a passive verb) is delicate. Someone can end up victimized when the balance is broken.

In a broader way correctional workers need to take care of themselves. This means not putting their persons at risk. We know of one retired Chief Probation Officer who regularly counseled his newly hired staff to "...get out of the district by nightfall." It was to his consternation and chagrin that such advice would fall on deaf ears. One young woman Probation Officer, ignoring this good advice, visiting clients homes long after dark, was actually held against her will in a ghetto apartment and subsequently attacked. She had truly become the victim. Although this is an astonishing case, we know of others, some more violent, some less. One woman volunteer became pregnant following a delinquent gang rape. She had come face-to-face with members of an inner city gang whose initiation agenda included the rape of a virgin. Unfortunately for her, she fit the objective; perhaps because of, and certainly not in spite of her identifiable clerical identity.

Less ugly recounts are abundant. A viewing of the film "Youth Terror: View Behind the Gun" (BAVI:1978) reveals a robbery in progress; the victim was the young reporter conducting the interviews for the documentary. So we see that such situations occur in the most unpredictable of circumstances. We are particularly dismayed when colleagues sometimes refer to such delinquent behavior as "rites of passage." Such attempts demean the victim and trivialize the concept of violent crime.

Probably the most notorious case of victimization in recent years where young delinquents themselves became victims was that of the four young black teenagers who were shot by Bernhard Goetz. This occurred on the New York subway and national media coverage followed for several months. The story was that the four confronted the adult white male and "asked" for five dollars. Whatever went on between them, Mr. Goetz had a pistol; he ended up permanently crippling one, while seriously wounding the other three. Much debate over this type of vigilantism raged in the press and among both conservatives and liberals of academia. Although it would appear the Courts did not come down hard on Goetz, public opinion seemed *not* to support his actions. The case, though, raised the troubling spectacle of an armed citizenry violently reacting to the perceived threat of community lawlessness. If nothing less, the incident became a metaphor for urban crime and individualism personified.

The Audience as Decision Makers: Significant Others.

The one observation that can be made about college and university teaching is that someday, sometime in the future, our students will become prime movers. They will sit on school boards, city councils, county boards; they will be elected to public office at the local, state and even national level. Those who do not will be a part of the influence that is wielded for action and accounting. At the very least, this is the way it is supposed to work in a democracy. We have faith that it will.

To that end, the professoriate on university campuses nationwide must constantly re-evaluate and update curricula. Anyone familiar with the current state of educational affairs has no doubt that considerable dialogue is now taking place. As the turn of the nineteenth to twentieth centuries ushered in the framework for action and concern for criminal and juvenile justice that was to last for the better part of three quarters of a century, so too will the turnover into the twenty-first century bring about exciting change. We do believe this. Even though there are many problems that we see, and have addressed a few in this monograph, new forms are presently vaguely discernable. But they are there. More at the end of careers than at the beginning, it is with some sense of envious melancholy that we consider the future.

Those who are in positions of power today were schooled in a time past. It is supposed that the liberal agenda of those clinging to the rehabilitation model has its roots in an earlier America. The hope for the future is that mistakes of the past will not continue to be repeated. Surely we have come a long way. In pointing out some of the past community strain and obstacles to problem solving, it is our hope that the future will offer much compromise for the agenda of social change.

One group of persons that has had a profound impact on events, especially in the last two decades has been the legislators. Probably more so at the State levels of government, but also at the top and the lower end of Federal and local government. The events that have unfolded have significantly changed the relationships of the whole Juvenile and Criminal Justice system. This in no way of course minimizes the Judicial system where appellate reviewers can often be seen to be the prime movers. It was, after all, the Gault decision of 1967 that is most often cited for obtaining due process for juveniles in Courts of Law.

One Juvenile Court Director told a Juvenile Delinquency class of ours recently that he felt the most far reaching decision affecting the relationship between the Court and delinquents was that of *Gallegos vs. Colorado* (1961). In this latter case (Fox 1970:119) the Court is required to apply the "totality of circumstances" test when juveniles are being adjudicated. The meaning behind this is that the adjudicatory burden "tilts" in favor of the juvenile; the Court must consider the events surrounding a juveniles knowledge of wrong doing, ...and most importantly one of the considerations is that the juvenile *is* a child. Can a child ever really understand the process, what went on during investigation, interrogation, and so forth? A substantial argument can be made otherwise,...when taking into consideration that a child is, after all, still a child.

Our quarrel with much of the direction of the decisions to cloak juveniles with all of the rights in the citizens of a democracy, is that it moves the concern for juveniles toward criminal procedure. The Criminal Court is a court of record; the Juvenile Court is one of equity, summary, and/or chancery jurisdiction. In the Criminal Court the trial is a contest where the State is involved with the defendant as adversary. Due process rights are intended to make the contest fair; and if the defendant loses, ...well, that's tough!

But what about juveniles? If we gird them with all of the conceivable protection of the fifth amendment to the Constitution are they ready for an adult contest? (This is the article where *due process* is most often inferred; our reading of the actual words would appear to limit *due process* to *habeas corpus* and self-incrimination; maybe that's why social scientists are not involved in appellate review). Is society ready? It's a real *non sequitur* to claim that *due process* is insured because of the proliferation of the public defender's offices. What happens if and when the juvenile looses in Court? Can we then say; "Oops!..,"...best out of three!" That is not the way Courts of record work!

Several decades ago the late Donald Taft commented that it was his prediction that the Criminal Courts would become much more like the Juvenile Courts. He thought that the procedures of the Criminal Court would become less adversarial, and take on the benign concern for justice that he felt was embodied in Juvenile Court philosophy. Taft could not have been more mistaken. It has been the other way around. And most of the reasons for this are traceable to appellate review.

This sounds like we are antagonistic toward the judiciary and what has happened. We are at times frustrated. It is often disconcerting. But we want to add that we are totally in support of our judicial processes as they are evolving. As we have come to live with and accommodate the social changes surrounding juvenile and criminal justice, there is a sense that our system in its totality, is better than it could be elsewhere. One has only to read about world events, other cultures, other societies, other systems of Justice, to come to this conclusion. The very difficult task is to assimilate all that has gone on and to integrate it into the justice system. Compromise on the part of those responsible for worthwhile social change must occur.

But if it has been the review Courts that are at the starting point of recent rapid change, it is the legislative branches of government that have altered many of the ground rules under which the system operates. It has become difficult to keep up with the various codes that have been enacted at

State levels in recent years. The delinquency texts don't even make the pretence at keeping up, *albeit* generalities abound. Advising students who intend to make careers in juvenile justice, it is best to tell them that they will have to learn law codes, rules, regulations, and policy on the job. Hopefully knowing the history, philosophy and distinctiveness of the juvenile court will be enough to get them by.

Years back we were astonished at the amount of information that was produced by the various Congressional hearings on juvenile delinquency. Subcommittees were fond of traveling around the United States, setting up hearings in various cities. Friendly "subpoenas" were sent out to various officials who were employed in the Justice field. Testimony was taken and records were gathered, collated, and disseminated, ...mostly to book shelves. Year by year, volumes were published by the United States Office of Printing and distributed widely. We don't know of anyone who actually read these. They were impressive for their size. A criticism is that too much of scarce funding was being squandered. The suspicion abounded that these hearings were in fact mere junkets made by the legislative body at public expense. Purpose appeared obscure. In any event the information production took on the appearance of redundancy. Sophisticated knowledge was more readily available in the texts and journals, and at the conferences, seminars and colloquiums generated from the campuses, agencies and professional organizations.

One story that shows the legislative impact on happenings in the correctional field occurred some years ago. The various States define delinquency legally, starting with the dimension of age. For most jurisdictions a person can only be a delinquent between the ages of ten (10) and eighteen (18). This varies by State. Sometimes the upper age is the seventeenth birthday for males, eighteenth for females. Such was the case in Illinois. A number of prime movers, interested and influential citizens, once petitioned several legislators to even out this apparent discrimination between the genders; to make juvenile status the eighteenth birthday for boys and girls. We do not question the logic of this. But the effect was to place a whole new population of persons under juvenile court jurisdiction; all those boys who were in their seventeenth year of life. Disastrous overcrowding of facilities occurred at the juvenile level, together with intense pressures on programs and resources. The policy implementers in the legislature had not been in "sync" with those who were responsible for implementation.

Although the sudden downsizing of population and case loads must have been welcomed at the criminal court and county jail level, it was not without a great deal of consternation by others who were most directly effected.

On the individual case level one juvenile's story stood out.   A seventeen year old boy was transferred from Criminal Court jurisdiction to Juvenile Court.   For several months he had been an inmate of the county jail, housed under very overcrowded conditions with an adult male population of very serious offenders.   In response to the change in age under which the criminal court operated, the prosecutors office (State Attorney's Office) summarily dismissed most of the seventeen year old's cases, deciding not to seek indictments.   Some few, as in the case of this seventeen year old, were sent to juvenile court jurisdiction.   A transfer from County Jail to Juvenile Detention facilities was affected.

The interesting part of this boy's story was the shocking revelation of his period of incarceration in an adult facility. He had been the object of sexual assault; his stories were vivid with the most outrageous of predatory assault imaginable.   When transferred back to Juvenile authority he was unable to urinate and had to be taken to county hospital and catherized twice daily. This lasted for about two weeks. He eventually recovered physically. The juvenile authorities were most incensed with the affair, reporting it through official channels to the State prosecutors and Warden of the county jail. Nothing was done. The messages that came back were that this case was not at all unusual.

Though we are aware of this reality of our penal system, we never cease to be astonished.   Our liberal backgrounds often lead us to conclude that things cannot be all as bad as reported.   They are!   Indeed they are!

Perhaps George Will's critique of the liberal's *forte*, that very liberal belief in the dignity of man, is appropriate here.   Will once wrote of his astonishment   "...at the recuperative power of innocence."   He was referring to the habit of Liberals to forgive and forget, to forgive and forget, to...*ad finitem.*[3]

We want to believe that people can get along together; we want to trust, and to hope in the presence of human dignity. Perhaps taking heart from the writings of the New Testament would help: "I do believe. Help me overcome my unbelief." (Mark 9:24)

Terrifying as this case may seem, it certainly bolsters the position of the "scared Straight" programs around the United States. Starting at Rahway Prison somewhat over a decade ago, the idea was put forward that young delinquents could be turned around in their deviant careers by exposing them to a day within the prison confines, taunted by adult inmates. Scaring them straight as a program took on life of its own. Most of the verbal abuse had sexual overtones.   Though we are extremely uncomfortable with these approaches to controlling delinquency and crime, such programs have proliferated.   There is a similar Scared Straight venture at Waupun, Wisconsin.

And although much of the very verbally aggressive inmate behavior has been muted, a similar program exists at San Quentin State Prison in California. There it is called the "Squires Program," and the objective appears to be about the same as "Scared Straight" with the exception that it is much less *visceral*; the inmates interact with the young people who are brought to the Prison more *cognitively*; they leave out most of the emotional overtones of what happens in the place.

Our advice on the matter of these programs is to steer clear of them. There are not only serious legal liabilities that may attach, there are equally serious moral implications.   Legally, the authorities are responsible for anything going wrong. A visiting juvenile to such a program could get very seriously hurt, both physically as well as emotionally.

And if anyone should feel that pornography is morally offensive, the scared straight programs offer critical evidence.   We cannot under any circumstances envision casework practitioners engaged as the inmates are with young persons. It would be considered reprehensible and not tolerated by colleagues in the correctional field. The underlying message seems to be that it is "OK" for the Scared Straight programs as long as (perhaps because) the adult prisoners conducting the taunting program (sideshow) are somehow not completely "responsible." We have been schooled with the imperative that *responsibility cannot* be delegated!

Another criticism of "scared straight" programs is their obvious attack on the adult facilities. Perhaps they deserve it, they do need to improve, to straighten up their act, and provide safety. Legislatures must provide the necessary backing however. This is the State's responsibility.

We would hate to be the Program Director at any State prison that also had a scared straight agenda. How could he possibly justify requests for funding for other institutional ventures? Outsiders could easily conclude that there is nothing worthwhile in these places.

There are many other decision makers who we would view as part of our audience to delinquency. Sometimes they are private persons, as was so in the instance of Jane Addams at the turn of the last century. More often than not they occupy a position of public trust, ...a Sheriff, a Judge, a particular Warden, Chief Probation Officer, an Alderman, or even some community leader that has taken on some kind of quasi-official status. This can happen and we have been witness to it. We have in mind two particular persons of the past: Saul Alinsky and Joseph Lohman.

Saul Alinsky was never particularly interested in crime and delinquency, preferring to spend much of his effort organizing the poor for action on their own behalf. His concerns were primarily in the areas of poverty and related discrimination. Although Alinsky has been deceased for many years, the Alinsky method of confrontation is still widely recognized. He was a community organizer, and he pre-dated the kind of civil right activism that became his hallmark. Many have sought to follow in his path. We have no doubt that his influence has been felt not only at the community levels, but also at the institutional.

There are many correctional systems that have formalized the processes of grievance supplication. At San Quentin Prison there are a wide array of procedural avenues where inmates can seek redness from perceived affront. This does not always sit well with the staff. Most employees of the system believe that inmates have no rights to complain. And yet the processes and procedures are in place.

Demographic and educational changes that have taken place in the United States during the last several decades will usher in a different prison population in the years to come. Though prison and juvenile facilities populations have had notoriously low levels of educational backgrounds, it is evident that they are changing. Inmates are bound to have more access, not only to the general information of the mass media, but also to the information that counts in their lives--the laws, the media reports on similar situations as their own and the like. Our own astonishment is that there is surprise on the part of authorities that the correctional culture mirrors the outside. Alinsky was a part of that change that brought about the confrontation that we see today. Some of it is not wholesome, but it is not without interest that new forms of caring for others, especially in correctional facilities, are emerging.

The late Donald Taft once spoke of the prison population in the United States during World War II. At that time many military draft evaders had wound up incarcerated. A large number of the inmates were the conscientious objectors to war. The Wardens at those prisons, together with their staffs, did not fully understand how to cope with this new breed of inmate. They were better educated and verbally astute. They originated from a middle class society. While we don't foresee a replication of this event today, the story is instructive as to what can happen when heightened levels of awareness, education and cognitive skills become common. Conscientious objectors of WWII vintage were as aware of their own civil rights and privileges as are many of the inmates of today.

The late Joseph D. Lohman had a truly remarkable and interesting career. He had been associated with the University of Chicago as a Lecturer in Sociology. However his main interests seemed to circle about crime and delinquency problems, and he always seemed to have the proverbial "many irons in the fire." He was consultant for many of the State and local projects, while simultaneously sitting on civil service examining boards, and guest lecturing most of the time. Perhaps he was involved in just too many kinds of activities most of his life. An impression of ours is that he was best in the role of social critic, wanting always to keep one foot in academia while being open to the implementation of the new things that were going on at the local, State and national levels.

It was in the mid 1950's that he had the opportunity to become involved in political life and public office. Chicago and its larger political area, Cook County, had gone through several years of distasteful police and political corruption. Lohman had always been somewhat close to the Democratic Party politics of Chicago, and he was slated to run as a reform candidate for the office of Sheriff.

Now in Cook County at that time, the Sheriff's office employed well over two hundred Deputies, Court Bailiffs and others. The Sheriff was also responsible for law enforcement for an area which had a population of over five million people. This department of local government--the Sheriff's Office--had historic roots that were deeply entwined with patronage, corruption, politics and business. Joe Lohman was the ideal type of reform candidate.

Except for one dispositional hangover to which Lohman seemed pre-disposed: he was serious about reform. He was in no way the consummate politician. To paraphrase and quote from a turn of the nineteenth century Chicago Saloon keeper Alderman: "...Chicago ain't ready for reform yet!"[4]

Under the patronage system of employment, jobs and positions of public office are filled by a political *quid pro quo*, ...something for something. The unusual *quid* was democratic party endorsement for the *quo*, which was appointment to a job. This has always been a part of American politics, and the Republican party has been involved as much as the Democratic.

A strong argument can be made both against and in support of the patronage system. On the one hand persons can be appointed without any respect to qualifications; but on the other hand this system has been pivotal for the integration of large groups of ethnics. From the last century where the Irish captured the Police recruiting process, to the Black control of many of the inner city departments of government, patronage has been the driving force. Indeed, for Whites especially, but also for Blacks, a case can be made that patronage is an *ersatz* welfare.

Anyway, Joe Lohman was elected as Sheriff of Cook County, Illinois. But his power to appoint others as Deputy Sheriffs was severely curtailed. For the most part, his own personal appointments were limited to one, relatively minor section of the sheriff's office, ...the Youth Bureau. Less than two dozen appointments were involved. Most of the rest were held under democratic party control.

Lohman would have a difficult time implementing any reform or change in the Sheriff's Office. Since the main purpose of his office as seen from outsiders is law enforcement and crime control, he decided to use the Youth Bureau, with his control over appointments, to police much of the most visible part of crime and corruption. The newspaper reports of the time recounted sheriff police raids on places where vice flourished. From the far north to the far south of the county, the sleazy businesses were hit repeatedly, as with the proverbial "hot iron." His youth bureau was at the forefront of such law enforcement forays and they did attract publicity.

One suburban unincorporated place where there had been a long history of sleaze was Calumet City, located on the Indiana border but still within Cook County, Illinois. The history of Calumet City was that in the early part of this century, following World War I, various elements of organized crime had taken over the city's "main drag," which consisted of about three to four city blocks. All sorts of vice were barely masked. The Calumet City permanent residents deliberately ignored the evidence of sleaze, pornography, gambling, prostitution and vice of all sorts on their main street. The *quid quo pro* for the community residents was lower property taxes. This satellite community had made a bargain with the devil. A decade later a reform mayor of the suburb was able to chase the repugnant enterprises away, but not without extreme measures.

As an aside, cities that allow their place to become a haven for organized crime eventually pay a very stiff price. Most reputable businesses shy away from the area. Even though organized crime, when operating the sleazy businesses, do not like violence (it's bad for business!), the possibility,...

no, the probability of violence is part of the life of such places. Lowered property taxes that were first a part of the "arrangement" (sleazy business can be hit with high property taxes) are dwarfed when lowered property valuations are factored in. It is just not a good deal for communities to let themselves be used on the fringes of organized crime.[5]

Two incursions by Sheriff Lohman's deputies into Calumet City's trashy sin industry are interesting in their own light, but also are informative about the nature of the relationships that evolve among power brokers in the juvenile justice system. One raid by the Juvenile Bureau deputies netted, among others, two juvenile females. Both of the girls were under eighteen years of age, and had they been adults, they would have been charged with lewd and lascivious conduct. Furthermore, they were ethnic American Indian, originating from a reservation in Canada, north of the U.S. New England States.

Sheriff Lohman would have a reasonably significant legal case to press against the owner of the bar and cabaret, since additional charges of contributing to the delinquency of minors always attracted significant press coverage. The cases would be heard in Juvenile Court where more sympathy was extended to defendants legally defined as children.

The two girls did appear older, ...not necessarily wiser or sophisticated, only older. Court workers and records would describe them as "haggard."

The cases would have been complicated enough by themselves, when a further development was uncovered. Whether Sheriff Lohman's deputies were just "lucky" or were truly wizards at criminal investigation is debatable. It was found out that the Indian girls had started their journey to Calumet City in New York, crossing the eastern part of the United States, through Pennsylvania, Ohio, and Indiana. And they did not come alone. An adult male had accompanied them and had left a paper trail of evidence strongly suggesting that he was, indeed, their companion, ...their pimp!

This unraveling might have gone no further except the young "escort" was the son of an organized crime figure in Chicago. One from the very top of the echelon. Outsiders and court personnel referred to the Don, and *mafia*. Lohman knew a case that would be notorious; he was aware that he had a particular advantage in his attack against organized crime in the suburb of Calumet City. And the potential in good publicity for himself and his office wouldn't be unwelcome either. Lohman did have ambitions in the political world.

Around Juvenile Courts, the insider can always tell when there's an interesting case afoot. Usually the signs are subtle: a case held *in camera* (Judges Chambers); staff scurrying about, ...particularly staff who are ordinarily not so visible (e.g., typists from the pool, operating engineers, custodial workers (janitors), even the Clerk of the Court. Another sign: the presence of lawyers who don't look like they belong.

The case of the two Indian girls had a bevy of obviously well paid lawyers. At that time, when a lawyer was cloaked in a coat and cape fashioned from vicuna wool, sporting a homburg, accompanied with obvious subordinate staff of his own, with several scurrying "flunkies" and "gophers,"...something was up! They were *not* representing the girls, but rather the interests of their client, the bar owner, and by extension, the interests of organized crime. It was never revealed exactly who was the owner, although for legal purposes there must have been someone named. Organized crime was interested.

The long drawn out case was exactly that: long and drawn out, through continuance after continuance after continuance. At a time when the average length of time taken to adjudicate a case was about nineteen days, this case lasted over seven hundred days! Finally, after about *two years*, the case was dismissed and the girls were returned to their reservation home in Canada. The lawyers had been successful in inhibiting charges of contributing to delinquency. Their strategy, as always in these cases, is to delay until everything and everyone becomes exhausted and weary. It does work. The crime boss' son was never charged in the case, much less brought before a Juvenile Court judge.

One other raid on the Calumet City night spots may have had a connection; we're not sure. About the same time that Sheriff Lohman was involved as the chief law enforcement officer in the case of the two Indian girls, another incident occurred. Apparently the *method of operation* in a Sheriff's raid where vice crime was suspected, was to have several deputies fan out throughout the crowd of Cabaret customers. When something unlawful was observed, the Captain of the Youth Bureau deputies would blow a whistle, and arrests would be made. Usually the barkeep and the performers were arrested and charged; at that time the customers were sent on their way, unless they had involved themselves in some extra-ordinary way. Such would have been highly unusual and unlikely.

Now as previously indicated Lohman's Youth Bureau were his own, his hand picked *cadre*. Their backgrounds were such that all would have a degree in the social sciences; some were former students from his sociology classes at the University of Chicago. Such was the case of Captain Boone of the Youth Bureau. At least one other of his deputies in this bureau, while holding the baccalaureate degree, also had political connections. The son of Sheriff Lohman's Chief Deputy, he was appointed probably on both political and personal grounds. The Chief Deputy himself had democratic party connections and was on leave from the Chicago Police for a tour of duty with the Sheriff's office. Such connections of family and politics is neither unusual nor inherently bad. Sometimes it can be argued positively; other times negatively. Usually this type of nepotism is thought to be poor; but then again many cases can be shown where all concerned are served well. In this instance the young deputy Sheriff exercised extremely poor judgment on the occasion of one of the Calumet City vice raids.

As the story unfolded to the circuit of insiders at the time, immediately following the blowing of the whistle by the Juvenile Bureau Captain and the announcement that there was a Sheriff's (police) raid in progress, the young deputy apparently became excited and discharged his revolver in the cabaret. Fortunately, no one was seriously injured. But the shot did "nick" one of the dancing girls, ...in the buttocks. Fortunately she received a minor flesh wound.

The whole incident was an extreme embarrassment for the Sheriff's Office. The story had the unverified finale that as a *quid pro quo* arrangement, Sheriff Lohman reluctantly agreed to keep his Youth Bureau squad out of Calumet City's night places for the foreseeable future.

One of the most significant cases that Sheriff Joe Lohman is least remembered for involved the lurid murder of two juvenile girls. They were sisters, and it was referred to as the Grime's murder cases. The girls naked and frozen bodies were discovered by the roadside in one of the western suburban Forest Preserves of Cook County.

The case was important because of its legal and operational impact for law enforcement. Most cases that end up in textbooks are there because of appellate review where a legal precedent is established. These two were extremely significant because of the manner of their unfolding not only at the trial court but also by way of the tremendous publicity that was given.

The public, and the vast array of persons that are part of the system developed a new attitude toward confessions. Most attorneys have always believed that the accused in criminal proceedings is his own worst enemy, and that convictions are made by way of the mouth and words of the accused. Appellate review has attempted to safeguard the individual from himself and his own declarations where such declarations are truly *ignoratio elenchi* (uninformed rebuttals). The Gault case (right to legal counsel in Court for juveniles); the *Miranda* warning (against self incrimination); the *Escobedo* case (the right to counsel at that moment where suspicion has narrowed); the *Kent* case (right to counsel regarding Waiver to Criminal Court); these and other cases like the one referred to earlier (*Gallegos*; totality of circumstance test for juveniles); all have their impact in juvenile and criminal justice.

But there are other cases that fall short of judicial review and weigh heavily in the interaction of law enforcement, those accused of crime and delinquency, and the general public. The case of Bernhard Goetz referred to previously was one of them. Though the issue of armed citizens resolving their own conflicts by way of individual vigilantism remains unresolved, Goetz will be remembered for drawing national attention to subway violence and law enforcement.

Another case involving the four indicted police officers from the Los Angeles police department in March 1991 may well stand out for drawing attention to police brutality and black discrimination; whether or not it eventually is judicially reviewed and becomes legal precedent. The fact that it was accidental that a private citizen happened to be present, and happened to have a camcorder to document the involvement of over a dozen LAPD officers either committing (or failing to intervene) in a brutal assault of a black motorist will be remembered. National TV coverage of the event did more to raise an issue to social consciousness than many other cases adjudicated by way of appellate review.

So it was with the Grimes sister's murders. The Sheriff's deputies arrested a suspect in the case. An itinerant dish washer and vagrant by the name of Benny Bedwell was charged in what was thought to be a sex crime murder. Much publicity was given to the crime. For Sheriff Lohman and his office, this public exposure as the law enforcer responsible for bringing a culprit to justice would be enviable. After all, his office of Sheriff did not have the ordinary manpower and forensic resources available that the Chicago and Federal law enforcement officials had at their disposal.

Bedwell confessed and was subsequently indicted and brought to trial. The confession was a large part of the evidence against him. In court his attorney was able to "prove" that he was in Florida at the time of the murder, casting serious doubt on his confession.

The Bedwell case was important because it drew the attention of the public to confessions by defendants. Beyond all of the legal niceties of

Miranda, Escobedo, Gallegos, etc.,the public became aware of something that was common knowledge among police and others in the justice system. This was that when serious crimes are reported, there is no shortage of individuals who are willing,eager and available to confess! Police must routinely sort out and reject the perennial confessors; the difficult part of this task is sorting out the new confessors to the list. And the job is not easy in spite of the black comedy that can be envisioned.

Bedwell's case was dismissed. The story goes that Sheriff Joe Lohman felt that his office had the right culprit all along and that the case was lost in court machinations. Most insiders disagreed. But it was after the Bedwell case that more concern was given to the circumstances of confessing and the confessor.

In the remaining pages of this chapter we will address the conditions under which the audience becomes a part of the delinquency and crime script. Essentially this will be effected by paying attention to our modern urban culture.

Urbanism, Urbanization and Individuation.
"The classic formulation of how urbanization fosters innovation, specialization, diversity, and anonymity is Wirth's essay..."(Palen 1987:142). We began this monograph with a consideration of his contribution to sociological insight and theory. The life patterns that he envisioned, emerging from an articulation of the three factors of urban size, compaction of living arrangements, and variegated ways of coping were evidenced in new types of individuals. Individuals were becoming increasingly more free, not only of the social burdens inherent in past economies and social/political structures, but also types of individuals were emerging that were more free of material restraint and want.

It has been said that Wirth was the consummate cosmopolite. He was also an optimist. He was one of those rare scholars in the sociological discipline who very effectively combined research, teaching, and community interest with social criticism. Others of his stature were the late Robert Martinson and C. Wright Mills. Currently our " social critic in residence" is the indomitable Robert K. Merton.

Individuation refers not only to a process of becoming distinct from others, but also of becoming spiritually free of the demons that bind us together and still pull us apart. We know we are alone and yet are aware of our dependency on others. We know we must live together and yet are aware of our own uniqueness. (Ellis 1987:100-101) For Wirth the optimism of his insights was that urbanism as a way of life would get better and better. He was, after all, of the Chicago School of Sociology which was optimistic to the core, despite an overconcentration on social problems of all sorts. Such was not just a value judgement for Wirth. Today it appears common sense to value the importance of modernization and all that this would entail. Note that the very idea the of "Third World" orders carry with it the weight of an enigma; we can't quite understand why they don't function. As the antithesis of modernization, the third world is at the very best a measuring rod of progress.

Yet while urbanism as a way of life would be constantly evolving and getting better, we imagine that even for Wirth some ways of living would arise that did not particularly articulate with others. Crime and delinquency are forms of behavior that, while we envision them as unfortunate by products of urbanization, are better seen as inarticulate ways of becoming. *Becoming* to the social scientist refers to the processes of taking on social form and structure. Certainly delinquency and crime may work well and pay off for the individual deviant. The functionalist in sociology would point out the "necessity" of deviance such that the system worked. The conflict theorist in sociology would even be a kind of "reverse functionalist" and point out how the subject becomes the object; how the aggressor becomes the victim. But for all of sociology there is little disagreement that deviance of all sorts (crime and delinquency for our interests) is dysfunctional. The ways of life for certain young people simply do not articulate well for the whole fabric of community.

We have tried to argue that much of delinquency comes about as a misunderstanding of what it means to be urban. The individual is not born to be a city person. We come into this world one by one and each takes on a way of life that facilitates getting along. We depend on each other. We have common expectations as to how others react to and treat us. And all of this is reconciled in our interaction with others. The articulation (or inarticulation) depends upon knowing and understanding the assumptions and ground rules that we live by in a modern urban society. Yet the culture of that society is not entirely clear even when all goes well. For the delinquent the premises upon which action is built exist in an even more shadow-like world. For all sorts of social problems of deviance the definition of the situation must be made clear. We could say that the consequences should be known, considered, and communicated. (Mackey, Fredericks, and Miller 1987:66)

But since the definition of consequence carries with it the pejorative of sanction, we prefer to point to objectives and purposes of social interaction. In this way the rationale for urban ways of life as articulating in the modern world can be understood.

Some authors have pointed out that delinquents, criminals and deviants are not necessarily rational in the first place, that their deviant actions often are quite bizarre and that deviance is not deterred by way of social control measures. (Siegel and Senna 1988:84) We think it prudent to reject the totality of these arguments. Surely there are cases where individuals are best described as enigmatic. We know of some such cases. Yet how often is it that real purposes and objectives are only uncovered after pain taking care is given through careful social and life history examination. Even when our empathy (understanding) becomes clear in particular instances of delinquency, we do not necessarily sympathize. Our sympathy is withheld because we realize the misunderstandings upon which deviant action is predicated. We recognize that delinquency does not articulate for the urban scene as a whole.

What has been written in the past few paragraphs probably could be condensed. Delinquents do not behave themselves! How do they not act as they are supposed to act? Drugs and alcohol as part of the explanation are situational. Juveniles are not "high" all of the time. Miscues to behavior abound in the world. A real part of the problem for misunderstanding urban ways of life probably has much to do with the rapidity of social change that has occurred, not only in the recent few generational spans of forty or fifty years, but also of social change that has occurred in the last century, give or take a few decades. The reader of this monograph will probably live to witness ashtrays becoming as quaint as cuspidors; NO SMOKING signs as uncommon as ones for NO SPITTING! What adult does not remember the phone "party line" where small communities shared communication access, ...and secrets. Most younger adults and juveniles consider pizza and fast food hamburger places to be timeless.

Whether social change has peaked and the rapidity of change will level out remains open to question. This is an area of cultural progress that we seem unable to do much about. It is also an area where we are reluctant to intervene. We do *not*, after all, want regression, even though some writers call attention to a bygone era, nostalgically remembering the "way it was." Usually such memories are quite selective, with offerings of both good and bad depending upon the point to be served. We did seem to have less delinquency in the nineteenth century. But we also had city streets that in summertime reeked of horse manure, billowing brown dust and mud. While we complain of pollution, we still must remember that garbage disposal and the modern sewage systems are recent innovations to the City scene.

So if delinquents do not behave themselves, how is it that this has come to be? Another part of the answer to this, aside from its urban context, has to do with interaction with others. We have already broadly hinted at our displeasure at viewing delinquency as a social role. The roles one takes in life have far more permanency than what we see to be delinquent actions. Yet we would be the first to affirm the notion that delinquency is social. If it is not social, and there are cases where such can be shown to be the case, then the sphere of authority and interest belongs to psychiatry and medicine. Cases involving necrophilia, mental retardation, and chemical endocrine imbalance come to mind as instances where action is not particularly social behavior. We are aware of such cases but will spare the reader further stories.

But if the social role is too much of a social construct to adequately portray delinquency, what are we left with? The answer it seems would be that delinquency and delinquent acts are particular and peculiar social relations; fractured and inarticulate social relationships that have been adopted. Manners, airs of expression, guise and guile are part of the delinquents repertoire. These are learned in human interaction. (Znaniecki 1952; Goffman 1959; Matza 1969)

We will briefly turn our attention to some of the others with whom potential delinquents come in contact. Even though we have downplayed the concept of social role, this does not mean that such do not exist. Some do. Like the role of the teacher or policeman. Juveniles do interact with persons, some of whom are playing out their social roles. But if there are roles like these two, what about social interaction of juveniles with the elderly? Demographics and life expectancy are responsible for much pedestrian interaction with elderly. Such was the case to a far more limited extent even a scant generation ago.

Social Relations and the Generalized Other.
Psychologists have investigated learning processes where models or modeling was the method employed to link independent variable to dependent. (Prentice 1972; Sarason 1968) The kinds of commitment to social action that seemed to develop are closer to our sense of the interaction that takes place in social relations that goes on in everyday life. Still others (McCord 1958) have looked at the effect of whole roles and role models on delinquent personalities. Even when these latter become the focus of attention (roles and/or role models) it would seem that the social

relationships of the moment, the definitions of the situation that are brought to bear, are the behavioral consequences of importance.

We have witnessed many attempts to alter delinquency patterns through exposure to "good" role types. Recent parenting education as attempts to upgrade role models are a case in point. Surely the emphasis on house parenting in community shelters, the Big Brother and Big Sister programs have similar goals. Not to disparage these worthwhile endeavors, we would still like to call attention to the many, many social relations that go on in daily living. Teachers in particular interface with the young. Many opportunities are presented where socially correct behavior and its underpinning of values can be portrayed. The definition of particular situations are found and understood in such contexts, but only *if* and *when* attempts are made at truthful communication. Persons of western civilized societies are not particularly adept at communicating correctly in social relationships. We learn early on to smile and be silent. A decade ago there was a particularly astute popular song titled "Smiling Faces." In essence it was a poignant critique of American duplicity in social relations.

The Teacher as Generalized Other.

More than just a teacher acting out a role, the interaction with young persons is first and foremost an encounter with the authority and power structure. It must be formidable. How else would the social structure of the classroom be as it is in the United States? One has only to contrast and compare the unusual teaching situation with the normal or average. There is a general cultural consensus on what is average or normal. We do have ideas on the decorum of the classroom. Look at a class for the emotionally disturbed or one in special education for delinquent non-conformists and take note of the average or typical situation. You will very quickly observe many of the social forces in our society that make for (or unmake) stability and order.

Education policy is prone to separating problem children from the mainstream for widely disparate populations of young persons. We have no quarrel with this as pedagogical policy. It is impossible for learning to proceed in the presence of disruption. Intelligence, gender, race, and ethnicity do not seem to matter; at least not politically. If a child becomes a problem in the classroom, any of these background factors will not save him from being actually or effectively separated.

Social class backgrounds do matter; at least politically. It is the lower social strata of youngsters that are most often separated and programmed into special classes and tracks, whether they are troublemakers or not. This can and does occur in the most subtle of ways. For the most part Americans reject the notion that we have a class based society. Ask especially any college group of students about their class backgrounds: they will tell you that they are *all* middle class. It is probably in such a lowered state of social class consciousness that there is such an easy acceptance by students and parents of separation and differentiation for educational purposes. (Babbie 1988:125)

What happens when an upper strata youngster is identified as a troublemaker? We are not sure this can be effectively answered here because it has deep political roots. Where it has recently become appropriate (the CW or conventional wisdom) to possess, to talk, to write, to think, and dialogue about politically correct speech, the reader will notice an absence of witticism where social class backgrounds are concerned. Race, politics, religion, sexual preference, gender, and ethnicity, ...these are not spared.

We looked at the social class backgrounds for a similar grouping of identified troublemakers several years ago in LaCrosse, Wisconsin. Although the school district did not have a special school for the socially maladjusted, the school principal had set aside one classroom where such students were placed; the rest of the school students moved from classroom to classroom during different periods of the day for different subject matter. All of the twenty-four students had been identified as troublemakers by the school faculty. Employing a standard stratification instrument (Hollingshead 1965) the twenty-four students were rank-ordered as to class backgrounds: the result: *all* were at the very, very bottom of the social index; none even approached middle class assignment on the basis of the inventory. Although this did not surprise us, our astonishment was at the surprise that the faculty and principal expressed. They had thought the group of pupils had been a more reasonable cross-section of the community, or at the very least of the school population. It wasn't.[6]

We have recollection of one story about the opening class days in September at the Montefiore School for the socially maladjusted in Chicago. The habit of the school district was to pluck out all of the troublemakers from the many grammar and high schools from the city school district. They were then transferred and assigned to the one location near Halstead and fourteenth streets.

At the Montefiore School in Chicago, one teacher once told us "...have you ever seen a class full of Chiefs and no Indians?" The class size for this socially maladjusted group was limited to twenty-four.

It seems that on opening day each year the classroom populations would be all new; new to the teacher and new for the students. All were from a different parts of the city. Each pupil was a leader at his old school and from his old neighborhood. The beginning social structure of the classroom situation at this school for the socially maladjusted involved all leaders: no followers. Assignment to the school on the basis of being an identified troublemaker took on the added dimension of being a leader. Actually this was no surprise.

It took the better part of six to eight weeks for a rearrangement of the interaction to occur. By then a new hierarchy would develop. New leaders; new followers! Such an arrangement always had the kind of tentativeness attached that history reminds us was par for the course in the band and tribal society of the American Indian. Fighting and violence, jockeying for position and power was most often the order of the day. Elman Service indicated that "...the threats of violence caused by the ego demands of individuals are countered by social demands of generosity, kindness, and courtesy. What the philosophers did not consider was that a society without governmental forms was still not in a state of freedom." (1975:48)

Teachers can be especially subject to criticism by the very nature of their work. They are close to young persons on a daily and hourly basis. Athletic instructors particularly come in close physical contact. Sound advice to such teachers is to beware of "hugs" or friendly "pats," or other physical expressions of communication.

We do not have to agree with this; this is the way it is in our society and culture. Teachers can and do become accused of brutality and/or sexual harassment. Legal counsel for the State of Wisconsin has told the State's teachers that a charge of harassment "tilts" against a teacher whenever physical contact is in evidence. Much of the time such charges appear trivial when the personalities of the accused and accusers are known. But charges like these are difficult to defend in open Court.

We remember one case where a gym instructor was accused by a young person who had been in custody awaiting adjudication on a petition charging violent delinquency. The staff and court officials had the unstated, gut-level feeling that the accusation was a distraction leveled at the gym instructor to draw attention away from the more serious matter before the Court. The boy was accused of serious delinquency; the Prosecutor's office was looking for waiver to Criminal Court and indictment by the sitting Grand Jury. As indicated before, such cases are difficult to defend or resolve.

How is it proved, how is it brought into evidence that an infraction did *not* occur?   In the absence of physical injury, where is the proof that harassment or brutality has occurred?   Surely we know of instances where the argument can go both ways.   In the case of the accused gym instructor the conclusion in open Court was at best ambiguous.   Juvenile Courts, however, are likely to "go easier" on juveniles that make such accusations when it comes to their own delinquency charge being adjudicated.   Everyone involved seems to want to get it all over, done with, and out of sight.   Talking to an older prosecutor at the time, he noted the Lawyer's humorous stratagem of courtroom technique: "If you know the facts of a case, pound away at the jury; if you don't know the facts but you do know the law, pound away at the Judge; if you don't know the facts OR the law,...pound away on the table!"

Teachers as part of the ubiquitous audience are important as generalized others for young persons.   Teachers on the whole have been ill served by television and radio in particular, and the mass media in general. The roles that have been portrayed are trite.   By the time children are in the fourth grade they have begun to react toward teachers in the way that the general public, our society and culture portray them.   Our culture is duplicitous in this regard.   While pontificating upon and extolling the virtues of the teaching "professions," the public simultaneously disparages it. Undoubtedly it is the history of condescending rhetoric concerning teachers that encourages this.   "Those that can do; those that can't do, teach; those that can't do or teach, teach teachers to teach!"   "Our Miss Brooks!"   "Goodby Mr. Chips."   The Blackboard Jungle!   The absent minded professor!

Another reason for the public's quixotic attitude toward the teaching degree and career is that in the United States there has been a long history of teaching service that has borderlined on charity.   It was not overly burdensome for an elite rural society of the nineteenth century to encourage altruism in teaching.   American society did such a hundred years ago.   But is this feasible for the mass culture and society of today?   The institutions that supported education in the past are not viable for this purpose today.

It is with this in mind that we referred to the teachers unions in earlier chapters.   Institutionalized unionization in the United States still is in the formative stages.   If not only the teachers, but also their collegial counterparts in corrections (Agency Social Workers, Probation Officers, Institutional Staff) are ever to realize their career potentials it will be through collective action. It was Saul Alinsky, among others, who drew attention to the ineffectiveness of individual action in mass society.   Only through group action is purpose achieved in our modern urban world.

One last concern about teaching and the relation that is established with young people is over the kinds of interaction that take place. As indicated previously, understanding must be communicated correctly and truthfully in order that social relations occur that are not somehow deviant. Children need to know the ground rules, the assumptions upon which to base their action. It is our contention that most of delinquency occurs because young persons do not behave, and they really never have been taught to behave themselves.

A central concern in recent years for pedagogy has been over the teaching of self esteem. The concept has to do with feelings of self worth, feeling "good" about oneself. Authors Rosenberg, Schooler and Schoenbach (1989:1016) have noted the reciprocity that appears to exist between delinquency and self worth. Low self worth feelings can lead to delinquency, and delinquency can lead to feelings of low self worth. Even feeling good about oneself can lead to delinquency when social class backgrounds are taken into consideration. On the whole though, upper class children are more likely to be non-delinquent than lower class children if they have positive self images; perhaps it should be stated that it is *because* of their positive feelings of self worth. The research in this area is quite tentative and narrow.

Our recommendation for teachers is to be careful in their social relations with children until (and unless) we know more about self esteem and social action, whether that action is deviant or productive. In the absence of a broad theoretical system that tells us what is going on in social relations, we would urge that communication be forthright, truthful, and correct. All too often we have observed, that in the interest of trying to develop self esteem for others, particularly in teaching, young persons are given false clues as to their behavior. They are "passed on" regardless of adequate performance. Grade inflation did not just happen in a vacuum. We want images of self worth; but we also want reality to be addressed. David Matza seems to be saying the same thing when he addresses the concept of the "social work ethic." We noted this previously. By this concept he means that practitioners give a false sense of reality to delinquent clients, downplaying their delinquent peccadillos, all in the name of trying to establish *rapport*.

Also, our culture has the imperative that in social relations we do not draw attention to others shortcomings. We are advising teachers that they must communicate correctly. Many times this will be extremely difficult. But our youth cannot be expected to behave themselves if they don't understand the ground rules.

The Police as Generalized Other.

The presence or absence of law enforcement in the form of a visible policeman was a kind of short lived phenomenon for modern urban society. Hollywood versions portray the London "Bobby" walking erect, casually rattling the wrought in fence bars with his baton; or the Pat O'Brien films of the 1930's: he was prototype of the urban Irish cop. The neighborhood patrol officer, the "beat" cop, lasted in that role until just after World War II ended. Today such is an anachronism. This is too bad. We would not argue for the return of the neighborhood policeman. It's just not going to happen for many reasons. Cost effectiveness is just the first. Performance effectiveness is another; mobility is just too important in today's society.

Those who argue for a police presence, a visible police officer, are proactive in criminal justice. That such visibility deterred the commission of crime is an assumption based on an idea of a particular type of society. We tend to forget or downplay the kind of society we were when the cop walked his inner city beat. It is doubtful that meaningful re-enactment could occur; places within cities where the need would be greatest are just too dangerous today.

Yet there is a longing for the reassurance of a police presence. We know of a small city in northwest Wisconsin that hired a twelfth grader, a seventeen year old boy, to wear a police uniform and drive their police squad car around town after school. We know of a far south west Florida city that hired an eighty-plus year old senior citizen to sit in uniform by the Beach pier. We know of an IGA food and liquor store owner who hung a police officer's jacket in the back of the store, clearly and pointedly visible to the customers. Such "pro active" crime prevention is about as good as the concave (fish-eye) mirrors, rotating TV cameras, and overly obvious one-way mirrors found in department stores. What can we say? They're better than nothing and they are low budget.

It would seem to us that proactive police work should focus on people rather than on hardware and superficial symbols. Symbolic manipulations are satisfactory as far as they go, but it would seem to be better if the symbols were part of everyday life. Such was the case of the uniformed policeman of yesteryear. One author, addressing the Black policeman in our modern urban society noted that nowdays as compared to a remembered past, Black police officers return home following their tours of duty carrying their uniforms in paper bags. His point was that the role, the job, and the position of Policeman had lost its dignity and its heart. (Alex 1969)

Schlossberg also noted a similar disparagement of the police role and its symbols:

> "Before now, policemen looked on their profession almost as a calling--like joining the priesthood. But as they feel less and less special, as they begin to have to accept the idea that theirs is just another job, the romance, the glory, the commitment will go out of the job. And in the long run the public will be the loser." (1976:44)[7]

As with teaching, where John Dewey taught us to pay attention to what the pupil should be doing, *not* the teacher, so do we call attention to what should be done by the individual policeman. This will eventually translate into meaning for the general public, the audience to delinquency. We recognize that this will not be easy. For anyone who has worked in correctional institutions, the point is that the *watchers* (the audience) must become more pro active. They do not simply occupy a status; they play a part. Young persons and potential delinquents will recognize when the situation is vacuous. To do otherwise is to set up confrontation and conflict in social relations.

Ever since World War II much consideration has been given to the "upgrading" of police personnel. Usually this means that officers ought have more formal education. It is debatable whether or not police ought to reflect the community they serve in educational backgrounds or whether or not they ought to be superior in such regards. Some California communities have made the college degree essential to employment. As we will note, this upgrading does not always ensure quality. We know of one Police Chief in a mid west city who once told us that he considered College education to "... ruin a good cop!" Though we disagree, we understand where he was coming from.

It is reminiscent of the old retired Sheriff who wrote about his days when the West was truly wild. That Sheriff wrote that it was the "...bad guy who always had the edge. He didn't have to think before he shot... anytime,... anything,... anyone." The Police Chief thought that college courses, particularly sociology, taught the student to consider the delinquent or criminal too much. He felt that such preoccupation was at best distracting and at worst, downright dangerous.

Teaching criminal justice courses in colleges and universities over the last four decades, delinquency and criminology especially, we have always been impressed with the presence of active police officers as students. Our impression is that they do get better, as students, as concerned citizens in a democracy, and hopefully as policeman. We have followed a number of them in their careers and have never been disappointed.

On one occasion in a juvenile delinquency class we were discussing the human characteristics that we think necessary to work with deviant, juvenile delinquents. We asked the question: "What do you do if (when) one spits in your face?" We should not have been surprised when the officer student raised his hand to volunteer his account of such an incident that he had. "I hit him. I knocked him down the stairs; and the landing was twelve down!" After this interesting class discussion, we thought we had reached a vicarious solution: some police training in assertiveness. One of the universities where the authors of this monograph have taught has offered free courses on assertiveness management. Other types of free courses have been on stress management, burnout, and the like. These are mostly aimed at young professionals, especially women, but others could easily see benefit. We sincerely hope and trust that this observation is not overtly chauvinistic.

The pitch for the free University classes on assertiveness training was to pose a question: "What do you do when someone 'bumps' you in a check out line; when someone deliberately steals your place? Do you smile, fume inwardly, get made and tell them off, ...or what?" The correct answer is of course "none of the above." Assertiveness training would teach that a polite verbal reminder to the offender was called for. The reminder was to be a lessen in civility. We understand, as in the case of the young person spitting in the police officer's face, that this is different. But then assertiveness training takes a while to learn and we will not go into all of the possible extensions here. It can be learned, however.

We did note above that education is not a panacea in upgrading police. But it is a good start. Often times more education is called for to cure all sorts of social ills. The war on drugs; the war on poverty; the battles at alleviating prejudice and discrimination. It is hard to turn down the notion that more education can be the cure for social problems. Educators that we are, we find it difficult to down play this particular institutional thrust. But we are wary. Note particularly the Los Angeles Police Department's involvement (March 1991) in a racially motivated beating of a motorist. These officers were educated. California police are most distinguished in educational attainment.

Social science research has consistently concluded that there is a strong negative (reverse) relationship between education and prejudice. The more the education the less the prejudice and *vice versa*. Most of the research observations have been made with indices of prejudice: paper and pencil tests.

One would have to wonder if education had not produced more sophisticated respondents and that prejudice was not diminished through education, ...only the type of response. If such is the case, and we are not sure, which would be preferable: an "Archie Bunker" type who is out front with his prejudicial attitudes, or the "J. R. Ewing" who is most adroit at concealing his true attitudes and beliefs?[8]

Because this sounds like an attack on education it must be addressed. Back in 1973-74. during the height of the Watergate scandal, it was noticed that most all of the men around then President Nixon were lawyers. One thing that did come out of this sordid history of ours was that several of the top Law Schools in the country had called for a revision of the curriculum. Specifically, more emphasis on ethics and moral philosophy were demanded. We do not know to what extent implementation has occurred. We suspect that like many problems, the solution has died aborning. What can be deduced from this though is that college and university curricula must change. It is changing. Values, ethics, and morality can and must be taught to all of our highly educated people.

It is not only the public sector schools and the K-12 grades that have downplayed teaching of values. The colleges and universities are part of the process in education. There are probably two reasons why education in the United States has come up short where ethics and values are concerned. The first is supposedly the "doctrine" of separation of Church and State. Morality, ethics, and values get very close to that which the institution of religion calls their province, their domain. Some K-12 schools have attempted to "water down," to dilute to the least common denominator the various prescriptions and subscriptions to morality that would cut across religious denominations. We will not go through the multitude of failed attempts. We only note that as far as the teaching of values is concerned, the system is in shambles. Something must be done.

It is a wonder that the law schools have not had more impact here. Do they not have doctoral dissertations that address and attempt to solve the educational problem of separation of Church and State? The answer to this seems quite obvious. All of the problems here cannot be left to appellate adjudication.

The second reason why education in the United States has been found wanting in the teaching of values is quite different. If the doctrine of separation of Church and State alone was the cause of a flaccid and flabby system of teaching values, then what do we have to say of our private sector schools? They are very little different. The emphasis on thinking for yourself, that one person's values are as good as anyone else's. These and like emphases are at the core of an educational problem. Very little attention is given to reasoned judgement. We note that many Universities across the United States are currently evaluating and re-ordering core curricula and basic studies requirements for all prospective graduates. Surely something exciting is afoot in the educational institutions. Opinions correctly formed, grounded in logic, reason and rationality are worth while. But one person's opinion can very well be wrong, illogical, peripheral, and sometimes downright dangerous.

We write the above few paragraphs with some unease. We are not insensitive to the feelings of others. We are proud of our own liberal credentials. We believe in individualism but believe also that it is ill served in giving up to curricula where anything and everything are equally valid.

Peripheral Social Relations.

There are many persons with whom young city people come into contact in their daily lives. We have argued that the relationships are interim and fleeting. Most interchanges are social yet lack the degree of commitment that are to be found in social role relations. It would be wrong to assume that the same depth of exchange as found between mother and child, siblings, married couples and even close friends obtains for most of the social relations enacted in everyday life.

Theoretical underpinning for the consideration of social relations of everyday life is found in the sociological literature. The works of Znaniecki, especially his *Cultural Sciences* (1952) and *Social Relations and Social Roles* (1965, *posthumus*), and most of the writings of Goffman during his academic career are particularly insightful. Even though much of the literature emanating from the interactionalist school of sociology seems concentrated on social role behavior, very often we can infer, to read between the lines so to speak, references to social relations as distinct systems of interaction. Znaniecki used the concept of *incipient tendency* as a kind of relationship in the process of taking form. Another way of looking at this would be to say that it is a situation looking for a place to happen. It is these manners, folkways, mores, or whatever we would call them, that we want to draw attention to in social relations.[9]

Of the several *types* of persons most often encountered by young persons in urban society, we would like to consider three: the elderly; the clerical; young peers. The reader can undoubtedly recount many more.

Social relations and the elderly.

There are some in the adult population that can remember urban neighborhoods where the elderly were constantly present. They were in view of everyone, often found to be sitting on front porches, gardening in back yards, sometimes gathered with adolescents, story-telling and reminiscing about the past. One of the authors of this monograph remembers that on moving to a small midwestern city in 1968 (LaCrosse, Wisconsin) from a Chicago neighborhood, a first impression of his family (and this impression was shared with his very young children) was the presence of so many elderly. Of course the impression was one of relative numbers. "Where did all these old persons come from?" Again, surveying a neighborhood on a home-to-home basis in this same town, one unmistakable impression was the large presence of an elderly population. In this last instance, though, they appear not to venture outside the home as much as would be remembered in previous times.

Even when one would reject impressions as not particularly reliable or valid, the literature in urban sociology constantly reminds us of bygone times where neighborhoods were highly integrated with respect to generational populations. The elderly were in constant evidence and they interacted with the young. The social relations connected them to community. (Jacobs 1971; Sjoberg 1960:92-94)

Current large urban cities have disproportionately large numbers of the young. This is due in large part to the "booms" in population, both the "baby boom" and what is now referred to as a "boomlet," (the boomers having babies) but it is also due to the kind of living that has evolved in the United States in the very recent past. Job relocations, single parents, and social and spatial mobility have created situations where the elderly are someplace else. The elderly are proportionately missing from urban enclaves and neighborhoods.

Professor William Julius Wilson posited the concept of *concentration effects* and how this contributes to the *social isolation* of the urban underclass. (1987:137-138) The thought is that because there are large numbers of homeless, unemployed, particularly Black males, and street people, this concentration of the underclass heightens the sense of being apart from society. We note a corollary for our purposes. For those elderly who are still in urban neighborhoods, they too must be socially isolated. The young must appear to be omnipresent. The opposite, too, must be the case. From the standpoint of the young the elderly must appear as if "foreign." They are all strangers in their own community. Few would wonder that the elderly are so often victims of delinquency and crime.

Social gerontology is the study of aging, the elderly and related issues. These social scientists have observed a set of common principles that have been lumped under the general category of "disengagement" theory. One of their concepts refers to the "role-less role" of the elderly. This no doubt views the fragmentation of former roles that were once central in their lives. Yet the social relations of our culture and society continue to be viable; at least that's the way it is supposed to be. As the elderly disengage from their former roles, it must be equally disappointing that they have so little to which to turn. Even the social relations they grew up to accept and expect are fragmented. The elderly can no longer count on deferential behavior from the young.

This must be especially sad in the context of today's economy. On the one hand we read about the plight of the elderly for proper medical coverage, and in many instances for adequate income. Yet on the other hand we can observe "senior discounts" and other forms of preferential treatment in our society. Perhaps it is only at the institutional level that they are being treated well; perhaps we should say "benignly." The elderly are a targeted market. Banks, travel agencies, restaurants, and other organizations all have their "specials" for the elderly. But what about individual social interaction? We have yet to observe progress at this most important level.

Senator Daniel Patrick Moynihan once wrote of a "...history of revolutionary rhetoric in the United States" that militated against those in power. We would also note that such a rhetoric continues to inveigh against the elderly. Those old fogies and such. Maybe it is that this group *was* in power, is no longer, and is therefore fair game to be the butt of much of our pejorative rhetoric.

We will end this consideration of the elderly on an upbeat note. Demographics such as they are will insure that the urban populations will change in the early part of the twenty-first century. Perhaps the social relations that develop between the elderly and the rest of our society will improve. While it is overly trite to point out that we all grow old, this is indeed the case.

Social Relations and Clergy.

Religious institutions have always been a part of the equation where delinquency is concerned. They have operated agencies and facilities that have cared for young delinquents and for children in trouble since the beginning of the rehabilitation movement in America and before. Houses of the Good Shepherd for "wayward" girls, the Gibault School for boys near

Terre Haute, Indiana (this was home to Charles Manson at one time); Catholic Charities, the Jewish Children's Bureau--a top rung agency; Boys Town in Nebraska has in the past few decades specifically targeted problem youth. There are many others that should and could be named. They are a credit to our society.

But what of religion as it relates to delinquency? Most all text books on delinquency have references devoted to an exploration of this topic. The messages are mixed however. While it would appear common sense that religious values *ought* to insulate against delinquency patterns, the implications from research are not clear. This perhaps is in part a result of research design. We remember intake face sheets for social histories that inquired into the religious preferences and backgrounds of referred juveniles. Perhaps it was too simplistic. Almost all referred juveniles would indicate membership in particular faiths' denominations, and churches. It now seems clear that the questions prodded the answers.

These considerations address the institutional connection to delinquency. But what of the functionaries of religion,...the Ministers, the Priests, the Sisters, the lay ministers and the like? Whittemore (1991:5) has observed that the ministers in our society are the last of the education generalists. Specialization has been preferred paths not only in all of science but also for the practice of sociology. This is becoming increasingly so, as it has for psychology, social work and other social sciences. Indeed, it is probably the case that the religious are also becoming specialized for encounters with young people. Note the various institutes, seminars, and workshops that are put on in the name of educational advancement. We had a hospital chaplain friend once complain to us that without the educational credentials (psychology, sociology, counseling, etc.), he would not be allowed to continue in his ministry. It is reminiscent of four decades ago when old policemen were sent back to school for college credits. The thought was that they could not perform that which they were accomplishing for decades without it.

Concerning the social relations between the young and the clergy in our urban society, we are not sure that there is much noticeable personal influence. There were times and instances in the past where clergy played a greater part in the lives of urban youth. It has been noted that there has been an increasing tendency toward secularization in America.

On a recent visit to Ireland our impression was that there were social interchanges in that society that were more like America's before WWII. America's clergy seem more content to go along with the secularization trend.

So many are indistinguishable, preferring to go about their business in *mufti*. How will the youth know appropriate required social relations when they are unsure to whom they are relating? While we must agree that dress codes and the like are not everything, they do offer cues to live by.

Social Relations and Peers.

Most of the textbooks in delinquency have a chapter, and sometimes more devoted to the subject of peers. Usually the focus of attention is on groups, or more specifically on gangs. There are many youth who interact with one another in today's society. Compared to the many social relations that are important for youngsters, gang life would pale by comparison. All youth are *not* members of gangs, but from a perusal of the popular literature, the weekly journals, the tabloids, and the TV news coverage one would conclude that life in the inner city centers around this subculture. This conclusion should be placed in perspective. There are many more social relationships that impact on the youth of a community

As we noted in an earlier chapter, gangs *do* exist. They can be formidable at times, and they can be a social problem. Hagedorn cites an argument in Milwaukee a few years back where the conservative Chief of Police and two "prominent liberals" sided together in their denial of a gang problem. (1988:153-155) Hagedorn says the reason for this cozy relationship, this marriage of convenience was for the politicization of the agenda.

To admit to a gang problem would: a) strengthen the police role in enforcement, b) fuel the fires of racism (most of the gangs referred to in the press were Black), and c) force competition for scarce resource dollars among agencies that would emphasize gang behavior. Neither the liberal nor the conservative camp wanted this to happen.

This reminds us of a recent *United Way* concern that many of their member agencies were getting too involved in the treatment of alcoholism, which they were. Alcohol treatment is where the allocation dollars are attracted. "Needs assessments" studies were implemented to clear the air, and also to gather information that would quiet down the competition. Such Needs Assessment studies do indeed work to depoliticize, at least as far as the competition for scarce resources is concerned. It is indeed unfortunate that there is a politicization of agendas in taking care of social problems such as these. It would be much better that compromise and negotiation on agenda occur. There is enough work for all.

As to the social relations between and among youth, we realize that we do not know much about this interaction. We mentioned earlier that Matza had identified the concept of "sounding" among youthful delinquent boys. This is an encounter where each tests out the limits of verbal one-upmanship. This social relationship is "not supposed" to end up in violence; but it can. We need to know, understand and identify other types of social relations among delinquent youth. To do so would significantly enlarge our theory of delinquency.

We will now turn our attention to some of the conclusions and implications of this monograph. Public policy demands an informed citizenry. Solving some of the dilemmas we face from the social problem of delinquency and crime likewise demand our best efforts. We try our best. Our final chapter is an epilogue.

The reader has by now noticed that our chapter titles resemble the Acts of a Play. It is as good a collating technique as any other we have encountered in texts, in paperback monographs, and in long and short articles. We hope and trust that it has intrigued the reader.

ENDNOTES FOR CHAPTER FIVE

1. We feel uncomfortable pointing to the South as a region of the United States where it is imputed there are traditional values which may lead to deviant actions and life styles. It would appear however, that popular television "soap" portrayals tend toward this direction. It is as though Americans "love to hate" and yet "hate to love" the southern historical experience. All the while though, love, or perhaps attraction and fascination is part of the equation.

2. Commercials are beginning to come more under attack by consumer advocates. Note for instance the recent effort to force Heileman Brewery to withdraw its high alcohol content ale from the market (*PowerMaster*, summer 1991). Advertising by the company had targeted the young, male, black, inner-city population. Such markets and sales pitches can be that specific! Two Chicago priests, Fathers George Clements and Mike Pfleger traveled to Heileman's corporate headquarters where they attempted to draw public attention to the coupling of advertising and the issue of alcohol consumption by the urban underclass. Both were arrested in the confrontation, although the resulting negative business publicity quickly resulted in the ale being withdrawn by the brewery. (*Times Review*, LaCrosse:7/4/91, p.1)

The actual agreement by the company was to discontinue manufacture of the high content alcohol ale; the limited amount already manufactured would be sold, *sans* the targeted market being identified. A perverse twist to advertising, marketing, and mass mentality is that the limited amount still being sold became especially coveted, selling for as much as ten dollars per twelve ounce can. But the market had switched: it was the urban white males who were now competing for the high alcohol prized ale! (*LaCrosse Tribune*, 8/14/91;p.1)

All of this is our attempt to draw attention to the role advertisement plays in everyday life. Can anyone doubt it's pervasive influence?

3. George Will regularly writes a column for *Newsweek* magazine. He has been the American writer most able to take either side in intellectual writing debate. Over the years his style and competence has earned respect from even those who disagree with his sometimes very conservative political philosophy. Like Senator Daniel Patrick Moynihan, he seems to have an uncanny ability to hone a phrase, to seemingly create that which becomes anecdotal.

4. Chicago and Cook county politics have had a long history of

colorful politicians and fascinating tales. Paddy Bawler and *Hinky-Dink* McKenna were two of the city's early characters; the quote is attributable to Paddy and has become somewhat of a prosaic old joke.

Chicago's name itself is derived from the native Calumet Indian word referring to the ubiquitous "stink weed" (the wild onions) that grew most profusely along Lake Michigan's southern shore.

The description of Chicago as the "windy city" was originally intended as a derogatory epithet by New Yorkers toward the city's often pompous and always bombastic politicians. The term stuck but was sanitized by Chicagoans to become the city's heraldic insignia; high winds from the east and off of Lake Michigan pummel the city's downtown.

During the "boom or bust" period surrounding the nineteen-twenty-nine stock market crash, Chicagoan Samuel Insull's name would predate the rival for villainy that the contemporary Charles Keating holds.

Both their names became synonymous with the banality depicting the collapse of their intricately woven financial houses of cards. Insull even had a building erected that became known as "Insull's throne." (McDonald 1962:112) The ediface was built to face Wall Street and the Eastern financial establishment. Erected on the west shore of the Chicago River, the building visually takes on the characteristics of an emperor's throne. Keating's "Taj Mahal" hotel that he had built in the western desert probably cost more but lacks the imagination of earlier "skullduggery."

5. In the nineteeen-nineties Property tax reform appears to be a major agenda piece for State governments and their local counterparts. In the rush to legitimatize gambling and other economic fringe ventures as a source of government revenue, it would behoove the power brokers to consider the history of Calumet City, Illinois. That "...there is no free lunch" is not only an American cliche, it is also full of meaning.

6. A study of pre-delinquent youth was conducted under the auspices of a grant from the Law Enforcement Assistance Program in 1972 to estimate the effect of long term group counseling in the classroom situation. Twenty-four youth were identified as problem students by the teachers at Logan Junior high school (LaCrosse, Wis.) and separately schooled in the same classroom with one special education trained teacher; the rest of the school students rotated to classes and subjects throughout the day. Additionally, the twenty-four were group-counseled one hour each day for the fall and spring semesters by two professionally credentialed social workers. (To the consternation of all, the twenty-four identified themselves as "the nerds") Mr. Watson, the school principal at the time, declared in September that the program would be successful *if* even *one* student remained in the program at the close of the academic year the following June. He predicted

that all would be forced to leave the school because of teen-aged pregnancy or commitment to State juvenile facilities.

Five students remained throughout the two semester program. Experientially we do not consider it a success.

7. We would maintain that there are a number of quasi-professionals that have seemingly lost a kind of luster that formerly attached to their jobs. Not only the police, but also nurses, clergy, and teachers have witnessed a diminution of their social worth in contemporary American society. We are not sure of the reasons for this. It is clearly a disadvantage for both the individual and society.

Part of the reason must be due in part to a kind of secularization process that has been occurring in America. Not only for the ministry but also for the others mentioned above, the aura, the mystique, the heart (the Greek word *Arete*) appears absent.

8. In referring to the two nineteen-eighty's television series of "All in the Family" and "Dallas" we assume that the reader is aware of the personality portrayals of the central characters. Throughout the two series the character of Archie Bunker was developed to epitomize a working class bigotry set against enigmatic comedy, while that of Dallas' "J.R." took on the appearance of inherent and duplicitous evil in matters of prejudice and discrimination.

9. The concept of attitude appeared in the very early literature of sociology. Since sociology and most of the social sciences were interested in social actions and activity that was spelled out in everyday life, the attitude concept had a difficulty attached to it. The behavioral sciences have developed excellent measurement questionnaires, scales, inventories and the like to assess attitudes quantitatively. (Robinson and Shaver 1973) Some psychologists (like Cattell 1946; Cattell, Saunders and Stice 1957; Perkins and Reeves 1970) have even developed scales with a qualitative twist. One implicit assumption that was always present was that attitudes eventually ended as social action. Such was *not* always the case!

Znaniecki addressed this theoretical problem by introducing the additional concept (1952) of *incipient tendencies*. An incipient tendency would be *triggered* to social action when circumstances were defined with respect to the situation. Although Znaniecki did not write of any *triggering* process, such can be inferred within the context of his works.

6
Epilogue

We have ended our last Chapter with the note that our observations of delinquency in the urban scene resemble a play. It might be better to have likened the analogy to that of theater. Teaching interactionist or social role theory to college students, it is most propitious to call attention to Shakespeare's writings, especially with his reference to "all the world's a stage," and on this stage we are called upon to play many roles. Some of those parts played and acted out have deep roots; others do not. We recall a recent televised interview with the British actor who played the role of Henry VIII for American Public Television series. He recounted how he had "psyched" himself up to the performance by first deliberately imagining that he owned all -- everything and everyone in his sight. He added that he then imagined himself as the richest of American industrialists. Finally, after considering these few ideas for days and weeks on end, he indicated that he then felt ready to go before the camera to project an image to an audience of that 16th century autocratic monarch.

The above is instructive because it draws attention to the theoretical basis of a social role. The reciprocal of social role is status. It is impossible to have one without the other. Status is the totality of privilege; it is that which is earned through performing a role. There is more to it than simply this, but let this point suffice for now.

In previous chapters we have tried to draw attention to interactions of everyday life that have far less permanence than the social role. Role performances by individuals are formalized in the institutional contexts of family, religion, politics, the economy, and the like; as such they have far more staying power. Social relations on the other hand, do not exhibit the same resilience as social roles. While the sociologist views social relations as formalized interactions with others, behaviors that for the most part aide in interaction with strangers, convention and consensus would refer to them as: morals, conduct, behavior, habits, routine, practice, breeding, politeness, suavity, urbanity, affectation, vanity, mode, vogue, decorum, propriety, conventionality, taste, *savior-faire*, etiquette, form, and formality.   The conventional antitheses would also obtain: vulgarity, vulgarism, rudeness, boorishness, grossness, misconduct, misbehavior, coarseness, ill-breeding, rowdyism, blackguardism, barbarism, ruffianism, and ribaldry. All of these can be subsumed as synonyms and antonyms under manners, ..."good"and "bad."(Devlin 1961:175)

We have tried to portray delinquency as something else, something less than a role performance, and we have also been cognizant of Louis Wirth's admonition that urbanism is a way of life. Delinquency and for that matter many other forms of deviant behavior can be conceived as fractured ways of life, from coping with contemporary city living.

All of this is not to deny the existence of social roles. The roles of mother, father, policeman, priest and the like do exist. Previously we had warned of a kind of role-congruency fallacy (or incongruency, as the case may be) where persons who have occupied particular roles are preconceived as special and usually negative types: the "red-neck" sheriff; "the welfare queens, the 'lolly-gagging' teachers (and) the greedy air traffic controllers." (Daly 1991)   The social implication of this form of stereotyping is to target for blame. Experience has led us to de-bunk these myths. Persons acting in roles indelibly put the stamp of their own selves in interaction with others.

There are several reasons for wanting to conceive delinquency as particular social relations and ways of life. First, common sense indicates that most forms of delinquency are just that, fractured social relations. We have never yet observed the delinquent in a role performance. Their actions are directed to the situation. It is true that there are "hard core" delinquents. There are also hard core alcoholics; but is there the social role of alcoholic? Cases that we have recounted in this monograph were *not* delinquent social role performances. The cases depicted were inarticulate ways of behaving with reference to coping in community living. This in no way detracts from the sometimes very serious nature of offenses against persons and property.

Second, in focusing on delinquency as bad manners and as impaired social relations, it would seem that it is a social problem that we can more directly attack. People can be taught to behave themselves with good manners and civility. Presently in American culture and society it is said that this task is up to the parents; that civility should be taught in the home. We would argue that the contemporary urban scene has become too complex to rely on the family institution for this task. As Harvey Cox and others of the 1960 *genre* challenged the religious institutions' vigor, vitality and viability by reference to "...God is dead," (1965:241-269) through extended analogy we point out that the family hearth fire is smoldering.

It is not necessary to enter into a protracted debate on this matter. While both sides of the question of family viability have their champions, one aspect of the argument not addressed is the subtle acceptance that parents can do something about the cultural impact on offspring, ... if only they tried harder! As a for-instance,... does anyone take seriously the ubiquitous television warning that "parental discretion is advised!" Pedestrian consensus has it that this media admonition is nothing more than a commercial ploy. It is a kind of "washing of the hands" in a disclaimer of commercial responsibility.

Third, by attempting to solve delinquency problems by exposure to good role models we are really kidding ourselves. While it is theoretically possible to do so in the one-on-one relationship, practicalities do not make this feasible for an assembly line endeavor. Even where such one-on-one relationships are programmed for rehabilitative purposes, it is doubtful that true role performances can prevail. Quite a few authors (Yablonsky 1962; Matza 1964) have noticed the kind of "con game" that goes on in interviews by authorities with individual delinquents. What is missing in the relationship is the totality of status arrangements. Young delinquents see through the artificiality of forced and contrived relationships. (Empey and Erikson 1972; the Provo experiment)

A fourth reason for considering delinquency within the framework of social relations, manners and ways of urban life, is that this narrows the definition somewhat. A narrowing of the definition of a social problem tends to depoliticize the agenda, while a broadening of the definition tends to do the opposite... to politicize. In studying social problems other than delinquency, Ellis noted that "...bureaucracies work best when the problems they deal with are diagnosed as *individual* problems or pathologies, rather than as manifestations of deep societal or structural problems. An individualized diagnosis and definition... depoliticizes." (1987:173)

While Ellis was referring to the social problem of spouse abuse, he offered a fascinating insight into social structures. Some individuals and groups have vested interest in drawing public attention to a social problem. This can best be accomplished by broadening the reference or definition. To this extent the argument becomes political. This is not always wrong, but individual persons can "fall through the cracks" in a political stand-off.

When considering social problems from an apolitical or political frame of reference, it should be remembered that it is always a matter of degree. One could argue that all of man's actions are political. Therefore we would add to Ellis' observations that to politicize or *de*politicize an agenda is a matter of emphasis or degree. This is not unimportant.

As noted earlier, the rehabilitative model for treating delinquents employed as one of its main concepts, an heraldic message of "individualizing the case." Perhaps it was because of this that the liberal agenda of the early twentieth century had far less political argument than is seen today.

With the advent of the "nothing works" doctrine and other broadening references to delinquency generally, we have come to witness much more political argument. The subtle notion that everyone is or has been delinquent offers special fodder for the brush of the cartoon critique or the pen of the social pundit. Much of the literature in delinquency and crime purports that this social problem cuts across the social distinctions of class, ethnicity, race, poverty/affluence and the like. The definition and perspective was effectively broadened.

While we do not believe that serious students of Juvenile and Criminal Justice would ascribe to the idea of random scatter of this social problem, much of the general public do believe this to be the case. Certainly such a belief politicizes the problem. An unfortunate by-product of this belief is that the solution(s) to the problem(s) is made to seem farther and farther away. For this reason (among others) we previously introduced the concept of *normative dispersion*. Social relations are social behaviors and they do have patterns other than being randomly scattered in society. Delinquency is one of a set of dispersed norms, social relationships, urban ways of life, that do not fit well.   In terms of community welfare, delinquency adds to our non-agreement on central community values. It is a disensus of the social order.

In Chapter four we addressed the principle of subsidiarity. Essentially the meaning of this guidepost to implementing social action is this: power and authority ought be decentralized as far as the general welfare will permit. The key to this definition is, of course, the conceptualization of general welfare. Yet after all of the arguments are heard concerning whose welfare must be taken into account, we do believe that the general welfare is NOT so abstract that it cannot be operationalized. To operationalize means to define in such a way so as to empirically verify. In other words, men of good will do know, understand, and agree on the essential characteristics of community well being, ...the common good. The common good and general welfare are operationalized by way of community consensus. This is a little reminiscent of Durkheim's "collective representation." For Durkheim the social act is a collective representation of what people believe and agree upon.

Our suggestion is that the principle of subsidiarity should be taken into consideration in the formation of public policy that addresses the delinquency problem; with one exception. Rather than focusing on decentralization of power and authority towards the individual and away from the broader community, we would urge centralizing that perspective or focus. The principle as it currently stands urges that the individual person be left to his own solutions in coping with life, yet consistent with the common good. If the common good is left wanting, the individual ought be helped by family. If the common good is still unfulfilled, then the local neighborhood, community or whatever ought fill in the gaps.

This process of decentralization of power and authority to act for the individuals welfare is always being centralized, concomitant with the common good and general welfare. The principle urges pressure toward decentralization and individualization.

Our suggestion toward centralization of power and authority to act in the best interests of the person does no structural harm to the principle. It only would cause the perspective to be shifted toward community action as opposed to individual. The general welfare and common good must still be taken into account. At the extreme, agreement is still operative that the State or the Federal Government ought not attempt to solve all social problems, especially in the case of delinquency and crime.

The reader might now ask: would this emphasis toward centralization of action for the welfare of individual delinquents tend to politicize the agenda for social change? It is a fair question and one which we ask ourselves. The answer would seem to be *NO!* Provided of course that due attention is given to our common good. We do believe that less politics would prevail. Such an effort on the behalf of our delinquent youth would be more in line with the "self help" thesis that is so commonly invoked when calling for "just deserts" for offenders. And still it would offer a framework where rehabilitation *could* work.

We have hope and trust that those responsible for the implementation of public policy will be able to compromise among themselves. Too many factions are engaged in confrontation over what to do about crime and delinquency. There is enough work for all of those responsible in the practice of corrections, juvenile and criminal justice. There can be a middle ground toward which a compromise can be made between those calling for a return to the rehabilitative model and those calling for "just deserts." The former (the old liberals) and the latter (the new liberal and conservative coalition) need to compromise. We think that the subsidiarity principle offers at the minimum, a helpful hint. The present harangue over giving the offender his "just deserts" versus rehabilitating him, filters out to be an argument over who is responsible and/or accountable: the individual or the community. Reform of the aberrant human condition will become evident in the hands of the givers and doers.

Shireman and Reamer have noted that even Martinson relented somewhat when considering the "nothing works" doctrine. Almost timidly, almost grudgingly, there is the message that some things (programs) seem to work,...under some conditions, sometimes, with some offenders. A lot of qualifications weigh in. These two authors present an alternative in the squabble over "just deserts" *versus* rehabilitation. They suggest the idea of *rehabilitative opportunity*. (1986:Chap.5) The meaning here is quite clear; opportunity for individual reform ought be open to the individual. The idea has merit and should not be dismissed. But what of all those who opt not to participate in their own reform? We simply cannot turn our backs on their problems or the problems they create.

One point that we would like to make on the "nothing works" doctrine, and we are a bit queazy in making it, is the following: Martinson and others made their conclusion after a thorough review of the relevant literature. Fault was found with much of the methodological setup in studies reviewing the effectiveness of delinquency control and prevention programs. Where studies did not lack scientific rigor, the evidence suggested that very, very little worked to meliorate the problem of juvenile delinquency. Our point is that written reports approximate as well as is feasible that which occurred under observation and investigation. As Benitez spoke of an "alchemy of police experience" in defining evidence on the urban streets, so do we speak out about an "alchemy of practical knowledge."

We have observed that people do change. Some authors point out that maturity takes place, suggesting biological magic. Maturation and maturity are quite different concepts. The former is somewhat backward looking in that it depends on ancestry; the latter at least looks to the future in the social agenda of everyday life. We are more comfortable with the idea that interactive civility takes place over time rather than an idea that the genes program the events.

And we have also seen written reports that did not completely match up with reality. Shireman and Reamer also indicate that the nature of our hard evidence in much of the correctional field still depends upon the written report of the night attendant, the jailer in charge of the shift, and others who do not have the published research document as their primary concern.(*op. cit.* p.21)

We say we are queazy and uncomfortable with this. It is both critical and criticism. Coming from academia we have learned respect for scholarly activity. And Martinson was a scholar. If we cannot effectively evaluate from the literature, where does this leave us? It is a predicament. We can only urge that *both* the scholarly literature *and* program implementation get better.

In leaning towards experience, we have fond memory of a very old radio sit-com from the pre-television era. On being quizzed about the veracity of a story, the comic invariably intoned what had become an American cultural anecdote: "*Vas you dere Charlie?*" Perhaps we should call this the Baron von Munchausen effect in recognition of a generation of doubting and incredulous radio fans.

In chapter one of this monograph we gave a few recommendations. One was that teachers ought to concern themselves with teaching that which ought be taught. This is the essence of academic freedom. Social relations can be taught. We do not need whole role models for youngsters to imitate. Manners and morals are taught in everyday life. The classroom is the most dominant situation for most American youth. Of course it goes without saying that *all* those involved in the lives of our young people should teach correct behavior. We are addressing those persons in particular who have career stakes. Others directly involved are the social workers, the probation officers, the correctional institution personnel and all of those who come into the daily life of the young: all should teach manners.

The professoriate should teach the aspirant workers to the correctional field. Professor Donald Taft once said that "...*ought* ought not ever be said, except in the sentence ought ought not be said." The liberal agenda of pre-nineteen-sixties has come a long way since that time. It is one of the least tenets of ideology that can modified.

We have faith that manners can be taught. When it is said that correctional institutions do not teach, the real message is that they do not teach what ought be taught. In actuality they teach very, very well; it is just that we do not like what is being taught, and for good reason. In Belfast, Ireland, in the Falls Road district it has been reported that the community has taken a dim view of its errant and delinquent youth. Not wanting to draw attention to a Protestant Constabulary, the local Irish Republican Army has been following up warnings for car theft and other forms of delinquency by "knee-capping." Transgressors are physically held down and shot with low velocity pistols on knee caps. The Belfast medical staff and hospitals have the dubious distinction of being the best in the world for knee surgery! This does diminish delinquency in the community. It is also much too high a price to pay to turn out a community of cripples in the name of delinquency control or prevention.

The point is that we can do something about our social problems. What is the price we are willing to pay? Can we translate our efforts into civilized programs? America is wealthy and our dollars are a claim on social activity. A major function of the careerist in corrections is to rationalize treatment (not in the Freudian sense). Treatment must be made rational to an audience of public policy implementors. When the price is right, the public will buy it. Anyone who has lived through the first Russian *Sputnik* in 1958 will remember the surge in educational endeavor that followed. The same held true for education following WWII with the introduction of the GI bill. The Peace Corps following John Fitzgerald Kennedy's inauguration also had successes not imagined by skeptics of the time.

Can we invent a system of juvenile and criminal justice that is caring? All too often the training of science has been that of impassionate objectivity. Even when there has been compassion it was always the individual provider that exhibited the behavior. How can we formalize compassion and yet keep it from becoming maudlin? As we move toward the twenty-first century we recognize that greed, avarice and individualism hold Court with the powerful. Getting the government "off our backs," privatization of responsibility, and a host of political reforms, all appear aimed at transference of wealth or retreat into anarchy. Anarchy specifically denotes the absence of government.

It is neither that the liberals on the left are capricious nor that the conservatives on the right are mean spirited. It is that we have forgotten all along that Charity to our fellow human being was never intended to be more than an expedient and interim response to Social Justice.

ainsi soit-il,

REFERENCES

Alex, Nicholas. 1969. *Black in Blue: A Study of the Negro Policeman.* N.Y.: Appleton-Century-Croft.

Arnold, William R. and Terrance Brungardt. 1983. *Juvenile Misconduct and Delinquency.* Boston: Houghton-Mifflin Co.

Babbie, Earl. 1988. *The Sociological Spirit.* Belmont, Ca.: Wadsworth Pub. Co.

Banton, Michael. 1965. "The Fragility of Simple Role Systems," in *The Sociological Perspective,* by Scott McNall. Boston: Little, Brown and Co. (1968): 163-165.

Bartollas, Clemens. 1990. *Juvenile Delinquency.* (2nd Ed) First ed., 1985. N.Y.: MacMillan Publishing Co.

Benitez, Peter. 1990. "Hard Drugs: Hard Choices. Law, Order and Community." Feb. 10, Video Tape. Public Broadcasting. (Mr. Benitez was Criminal Justice Coordinator for New York City, 1988-1989).

Bennis, Warren, 1973. "The Doppelganger Effect," in *Newsweek,* Sept. 17: p. 13.

Berger, Peter. 1971. "Sociology and Freedom." *The American Sociologist,* Vol. 6 (Feb.):1-5.

Berne, Eric. 1964. *Games People Play.* N.Y.: Grove Press.

159

Bettelheim, Bruno. 1958. "Individual and Mass Behavior in Extreme Situations," in Macoby, Eleanor; Theodore Newcomb and Eugene Hartley. *Readings in Social Psychology.* N.Y.: Holt, Rinehart and Winston. pp. 300-310.

Bierstedt, Robert. 1974. *The Social Order.* (4th ed.). N.Y.: McGraw-Hill. First edition, 1957.

Bortner, M.A. 1982. Inside a Juvenile Court: The Tarnished Ideal of Individualized Justice. N.Y.: New York Univ. Press.

Bureau of Audio Visual Instruction (BAVI), University of Wisconsin-Extension, Madison, Wis. (Educational Film & Video -- Rental Catalogue) (1988, 1978, 1976, 1970)

Burgess, Ernest. 1925. "The Growth of the City,"in Robert E. Park, Burgess, and Roderick McKenzie (ed.). *The City.* Chicago: Univ. of Chicago Press.

Caldwell, Erskine. 1940. *Tobacco Road.* N.Y.: Modern Library.

Capote, Truman, 1974. *The Glass House.* (Film only) Learning Corp. of America.

Cattell, Raymond B. 1946. *Description and Measurement of Personality.* Yonkers-on-Hudson, N.Y.: World Book Company.

Cattell, Raymond B., D. R. Saunders, and G. Stice. 1957. *Handbook for 16 Personality Factor Questionnaire.* Champaign, Ill.: Institute for Personality and Ability-Testing.

Cloward, Richard and Lloyd Ohlin. 1960. *Delinquency and Opportunity.* N.Y.: Free Press (MacMillan).

Cohen, Al. 1955. *Delinquent Boys.* Englewood Cliffs, N.Y.: Prentice-Hall.

Coleman, James S. 1957. *Community Conflict.* N.Y., Free Press.

Constitution of the United States. Printed by U.S. Department of Health, Education, and Welfare. Office of Education; revised 1951; reprinted 1962.

Cox, Harvey. 1965. *The Secular City. N.Y.: Macmillan Co.*

Criminal Justice Newsletter. 1990. Juvenile Justice: Nebraska. Legislature Begins Shift to Community Sanctions. Vol. 21, Number 12. June 15, pp. 4-5.

Cronin, John F. 1959. *Social Principles and Economic Life.* Milwaukee, Wis.: Bruce Publishing Co.

Cullen, Francis and Karen Gilbert. 1982. *Reaffirming Rehabilitation.* Cincinnati, Ohio: Anderson Pub. Co. (Forward by Donald Cressey, pp. xi-xxiii)

Daley, Steve. 1991. "John Sununu: Steely-eyed Conservative," syndicated column from *Chicago Tribune*, reprinted in *La Crosse Tribune*, May 3, p. A-4.

Devlin, Joseph. 1961. *A Dictionary of Synonyms and Antonyms.* N.Y.: Popular Library, Inc.

Dressler, David. 1969. *Practice and Theory of Probation and Parole.* N.Y.: Columbia Univ. Press.

Ellis, Desmond. 1987. *The Wrong Stuff: An Introduction to the Sociological Study of Deviance.* N.Y.: MacMillan Pub. Co.

Empey, LaMar and Maynard Erickson. 1972. *The Provo Experiment: Evaluating Community Control of Delinquency.* Lexington, Mass.: D. C. Heath.

Festinger, Leon. 1963. "The Theory of Cognitive Dissonance," in W. Schramm, *The Science of Human Communication.* N.Y.: Basic Books.

Fisse, Brent and John Braithwaite. 1983. *The Impact of Publicity on Corporate Offenders.*, Albany: State Univ. of New York Press.

Flowers, R. Barri. 1990. *The Adolescent Criminal.* Jefferson, N.C.: McFarland & Co., Inc.

Fogel, David. 1979. *We Are the Living Proof: The Justice Model for Corrections* (2nd ed.). Cincinnati, Oh.: Anderson.

Fox, Sanford J. 1971. *The Law of Juvenile Courts in a Nutshell.* St. Paul, MN: West Publishing Co.

Gibbons, Don C. and Marvin D. Krohn. 1991. *Delinquent Behavior*. (5th ed). Englewood Cliffs, N.J.: Prentice Hall.

Gibbons, Don C. 1976. *Delinquent Behavior*. (2nd ed.) Englewood Cliffs, N.J.: Prentice Hall.

Glasser, William. 1964. *Reality Therapy: A Realistic Approach to the Young Offender in Crime and Delinquency*; publication of the National Council on Crime and Delinquency, April: 135-144.

Goffman, Erving. 1959. *Presentation of Self in Everyday Life*. Garden City, N.Y.: Doubleday, Anchorbook.

_____. 1961. *Asylums*. Garden City, N.Y., Anchor; Doubleday & Co., Inc.

_____. 1961. "On the Characteristics of Total Institutions," in Donald Cressey, *The Prison: Studies in Institutional Organization and Change*. N.Y.: Holt, Rinehart and Winston: pp. 15-106.

_____. 1963. *Stigma: Notes on the Management of Spoiled Identity*. Englewood Cliffs, N.J.: Prentice-Hall.

Greenberger, Rabbi Ben. 1991. from "Terror: A Fundamental Conflict," Arts and Entertainment TV presentation, Part One (February). Exec. Producer Peter Montagnon. Film Archives, Israeli TV; Movietone; UNRWA, Visnews.

Gubrium, Jaber F. 1975. *Living and Dying at Murray Manor*. N.Y., St. Martins Press.

Haeckel, Ernst Heinrich. 1868. *The History of Creation*. (1968: American Edition; N.Y.: Appleton).

Hagedorn, John. 1988. *People and Folks: Gangs, Crime and the Underclass in a Rustbelt City*. Chicago: Lakeview Press.

Hollin, Clive R. 1990. *Cognitive-Behavioral Interventions with Young Offenders*. N.Y.: Pergamon Press.

Hollingshead, August B. 1965. *Two Factor Index of Social Participation*. New Haven, CT: Yale Station.

Jacobs, Jane. 1971. "City Limits," 16mm film presentation: National Film Board of Canada; based on: *The Death and Life of Great American Cities*. N.Y.: Random House (1961).

Karmen, Andrew. 1990. *Crime Victims: An Introduction to Victimology*. (2nd ed.) Pacific Grove, CA: Brooks/Cole Publishing Co.

Kesey, Ken. 1962. *One Flew Over the Cuckoo's Nest*. N.Y., Viking Press.

Krisberg, Barry and James Austin, 1978. *The Children of Ishmael*. Palo Alto, Ca.: Mayfield Pub. Co.

La Crosse Tribune. 1991. "...One Great Brew for White Guys." August 14, p. 1.

Lindzey, Gardner. 1954. *Handbook of Social Psychology*. (ed.) Cambridge, Mass.: Addison-Wesley, Vol. I: Ch. 1, "Historical Background," by Gordon Allport; Ch. 2, "Stimulus Response Contiguity and Reinforcement Theory," by Wm. W. Lambert; Ch. 4, "Psychoanalytic Theory...," by Hall, Calvin and Gardner Lindzey.

Loomis, Charles and Zona Loomis. 1965. (2nd ed.) (Chap 7 on P. A. Sorokin, pp. 444-497). N.Y.: Van Nostrand Co., Inc.

Lynd, Robert S. and Helen M. Lynd. 1956. *Middletown: A Study in Modern American Culture* (original, 1929). N.Y., Harcourt, Brace & World, Inc.

Mackey, William J., Steven Miller, and Marcel Fredericks. 1989. "An Analysis of Some Theoretic Formulations of Florian Znaniecki," in *Wisconsin Sociologist*, Vol 26. Spring/Summer.

Martinson, Robert. 1974. "What Works? Questions and Answers about Prison Reform." *The Public Interest*. 35:22-54.

Matza, David. 1964. *Delinquency and Drift*. N.Y.: John Wiley and Sons, Inc.

_____. 1969. *Becoming Deviant*. Englewood Cliffs, N.J.: Prentice-Hall, Inc.

McCloskey, H. and J. H. Schaar. 1965. "Psychological Dimensions of Anomy," in *American Sociological Review*. Vol. 30(Feb.): 14-39.

McCord, M. and W. McCord. 1958. "The Effects of Parental Role Models on Personality," in *Journal of Social Issues*, Vol. 14, pp. 66-75.

McDonald, Forrest. 1962. *INSULL.* Chicago and London: University of Chicago Press.

McLuhan, Marshall and Quentin Fiore. 1967. *The Medium Is the Massage.* Random House.

Merton, Robert and Robert Nisbet. 1961. *Contemporary Social Problems.* N.Y.: Harcourt, Brace and World, Inc.

Miller, Delbert C. 1963. "Town and Gown: The Power Structure of a University Town." *Am. Journal of Sociology.* Chicago: Univ. of Chicago Press, Jan. pp. 432-443.

Miller, Jerome. 1989. "Criminology: Is Rehabilitation a Waste of Time?" The Washington Post (4/23/89).

_____. 1989. "Is Rehabilitation a Waste of Time?" in *The Washington Post--Outposts*: April 23, 1989. C3:1-3.

Miller, Walter B. 1958. "Lower Class Culture as a Generating Milieu of Gang Delinquency," in *Journal of Social Issues*. Vol. 15: 5-19.

Mitchell, Margaret. 1966. (c1936). *Gone With the Wind.* N.Y.: Pocketbooks.

Moreno, Jacob and L. D. Zeleny. 1961. "Role Theory and Sociodrama," in *Readings in Contemporary American Sociology* (edited by J. S. Roucek.) Patterson, N.J.: Littlefield, Adams; pp. 642-654.

National Center on Institutions, 635 Slaters Lane, Alexandria, VA. 22314.

National Association of Volunteers in Criminal Justice. University of Wisconsin-Milwaukee, Division of Outreach and Continuing Education. Criminal Justice Institute, Milwaukee, Wis. 53201.

Neill, Thomas P. 1956. *The Common Good.* Garden City, N.Y.: Doubleday.

Newsweek, July 16, 1990, p. 63. "The New Teacher Corps."

Nicholson, Richard C. 1970. "Transactional Analysis: A New Method for Helping Offenders," in *Federal Probation.* Admin. Offices of U.S. Courts/Federal Bureau of Prisons. Washington, D.C., Vol. 34, No. 3, Sept.

Niebuhr, Reinhold, 1966. *Man's Nature and His Community: Essays on the Dynamics of Man's Personal and Social Existence.* London: Bles.

Niederhoffer, Arthur. 1967. *Behind the Shield: the Police in Urban Society.* Garden City, N.Y.: Doubleday & Co.

Palen, J. John. 1987. (3rd ed.) (1st & 2nd eds., 1975, 1981) *The Urban World.* N.Y.: McGraw-Hill.

Parsons, Talcott. 1958. "Definitions of Health and Illness in Light of American Values and Social Structure," in E.G. Jaco, *Patients, Physicians and Illness.* N.Y.: Free Press.

Perkins, Mark L. and John Reeves. 1970. "The Cattell 16PF as a Measure of Inmate Offense Type," unpublished paper; University of Georgia.

Poplin, Dennis E., 1979. *Communities: A Survey of Theories and Methods of Research.* N.Y.: MacMillan Publishing Co.

Poterfield, Austin L. 1946. *Youth in Trouble.* Fort Worth, TX.: Potishman Foundation.

Prentice, N.M. 1972. "The Influence of Live and Symbolic Modeling on Promoting Judgement of Adolescent Delinquents," in *Journal of Abnormal Psychology,* Vol. 2, pp. 157-161.

Puzo, Mario. 1969. *The God Father.* N.Y.: Putnam.

Riesman, David. 1950. *The Lonely Crowd* (with Nathan Glazer & Reuel Denney). Abridged, 1961. New Haven: Yale Univ. Press.

_____. 1954. *Individualism Reconsidered.* Garden City, N.Y.: Doubleday & Co.

Robinson, John P. and Phillip Shaver. 1973 (revised). *Measures of Social Psychological Attitudes.* Survey Research Center; Institute for Social Research.

Robison, Sophia. 1960. *Juvenile Delinquency*. N.Y.: Holt, Rinehart and Winston.

Rodale, J.I. 1969. "Does Sugar Make Criminals?" in *Prevention*. Emmaus, Pa.; pp. 107-114.

Rogers, Carl R. 1951. "Client-Centered Therapy." *Scientific American*. Boston: Houghton-Mifflin Pub. Co.

Roget, Peter Mark. *Roget's International Thesaurus*. 1977. Originally published in 1834 by Thos. Crowell, Pub.; N.Y.: Harper and Row, Pub. (4th ed.) Revised by Rob't. L. Chapman.

Rose, Arnold M. 1966. "On an Empirical Test of an American Dilemma." *Am. Soc. Review*. Vol 31, #1. (Communique)

Rosenberg, Morris, Carmi Schooler, and Carrie Schoenbach. 1989. "Self-Esteem and Adolescent Problems: Modeling Reciprocal Effects," in *American Sociological Review*. Vol. 54, No. 6. Dec.: 1004-1018.

Saint Mark. 9:14-32. *New Testament*. (New International Version.)

Sarason, I. and V. J. Ganger, 1973. "Modeling and Group Discussion in the Rehabilitation of Juvenile Delinquents," in *Journal of Counseling Psychology*, Vol. 20, 5:442-49.

Schlossberg, Harvey. 1976. "The Angry Mood of the Men in Blue," in *Time Weekly Magazine*, December 6, pp. 43-44.

Sennett, Richard and Jonathan Cobb. 1972. *The Hidden Injuries of Class*. N.Y., Vintage Books (Random House).

Sennett, Richard. 1969. *Classic Essays on the Culture of Cities*. (ed.) N.Y.; Appleton-Century-Crofts.

Service, Elman R. 1975. *Origins of the State and Civilization: The Process of Cultural Evolution*. N.Y.: W. W. Norton & Company.

Shireman, Charles and Frederick Reamer. 1986. *Rehabilitating Juvenile Justice*. N.Y.: Columbia Univ. Press.

Sheldon, William H. 1949. *Varieties of Delinquent Youth*. N.Y.: Harper & Row.

Siegel, Larry J. and J. J. Senna. 1988. *Juvenile Delinquency: Theory, Practice and Law*. (3rd ed.) St. Paul, MN: West Publishing Co.

Singer, Richard. 1979. *Just Deserts: Sentencing Based on Equality and Desert*. Cambridge, Ma.: Ballinger.

Sjoberg, Gideon. 1960. *The Pre-industrial City*. N.Y.: Free Press.

Snodgrass, Jon. 1982. *The Jack-Roller at Seventy*. (with Gilbert Geis, James Short, Jr., and Solomon Kobrin) Lexington, Ma: Lexington Books.

Sorokin, Pitirim A. 1965. "Sociology of Yesterday, Today, and Tomorrow." *Am. Soc. Review*, Vol. 30; #6. (ASA Pres. Address).

Srole, Leo. 1956. "Social Integration and Certain Corollaries: An Exploration Study," in *American Sociological Review*. Vol. 21 (Dec): 709-16.

Stein, Maurice. R. 1960. *The Eclypse of Community*. N.Y.: Harper and Row, Harper Torchbooks.

Steinbeck, John. 1972. *The Grapes of Wrath, Text and Criticism*. Edited by Peter Lisca. N.Y.: Viking Press.

Stryker, Sheldon. 1968. "Eulogy for Arnold Rose." *American Sociologist*. Vol. 3, #1 (Feb. 1968) pp. 60-61.

Tannenbaum, Frank. 1938. *Crime and the Community*. N.Y.: Columbia Univ. Press.

Taylor, Jeremy. 1989. "Strange New Science of Chaos," Public Broadcasting System. Video presentation. February.

Thornton, William E., Jr., L. Voigt and Wm. Doerner. 1987. (2nd ed.). *Delinquency and Justice*. N.Y.: Random House.

Times Review (La Crosse). 1991. "PowerMaster Protested by Priest Pair." July 4, p. 1

Trojanowicz, Robert C. and Merry Morash. 1987. *Juvenile Delinquency: Concepts and Control*. (4th ed.) Englewood Cliffs, N.J.: Prentice-Hall.

Trounstine, Philip J. and Terry Christensen. 1982. *Movers and Shakers: The Study of Community Power*. N.Y., St. Martins Press.

Vorrath, H.H. and L. Brendtro. 1974. *Positive Peer Culture*. Chicago: Aldine Pub. Co.

Washington Post. Oct. 28, 1990. "Crime: The Shame of It All." by Russell Mokhiber. *Review of Work* of John Braithwaite and Philip Pettit. C3:1.

Wheeler, Stanton and Leonard Cottrell, Jr. 1966. *The Labeling Process*. (with Anne Romasco). *Juvenile Delinquency: Its Prevention and Control*. N.Y.: Sage Foundation: 22-27.

Whittmore, Hank. 1991. "Ministers Under Stress." in *Parade* (*La Crosse Tribune*, Wis. *Magazine* section). April 14. pp. 4-6.

Whyte, William F. 1943. *Street Corner Society*. Chicago: Univ. of Chicago Press.

Wilson, James Q. and Richard Heernstein. 1985. *Crime and Human Nature*. N.Y.: Simon and Schuster.

Wilson, William Julius. 1987. *The Truly Disadvantaged: The Inner City, The Underclass, and Public Policy*. Chicago: University of Chicago Press.

Wirth, Louis. 1938. "Urbanism as a Way of Life." *American Journal of Sociology*, Vol. 44, July.

Wiseman, Fred. 1967. "Titticut Follies: A Documentary of Bridgewater State Hospital." Mr. Wiseman was Producer of this film, reviewed by participants at Reaffirming Rehabilitation II: Beyond the "Nothing Works" Myth; conference: Crystal City, VA. June 20-22, 1990.

Wooden, Kenneth. 1976. *Weeping in the Playtime of Others*. N.Y., McGraw-Hill Book Co.

Yablonsky, Lewis. 1962. *The Violent Gang*. First published, 1962, MacMillan. Reprinted 1972, Penguin Books.

Yinger, Milton, 1960. "Contraculture and Subculture," in *American Sociological Review*. Vol. 25: 625-635.

Ziff Davis Pub. Co. 1974. *Productivity and the Self-fulfilling Prophecy: The Pygmalion Effect*. (16mm film).

Znaniecki, Florian W. 1940. *The Social Role of the Man of Knowledge*. N.Y.: Columbia University Press.

_____. 1952. *Cultural Sciences*. Urbana, Ill.: University of Illinois Press.

_____. 1965. (Posthumus) *Social Relations and Social Roles*. San Francisco: Chandler Publishing Co.

Author Index

Alex (137)
Arnold and Brungardt (44)
Babbie (7) (133)
Banton (49) (78)
Bartollas (70)
Benitez (86)
Bennis (92)
Berger (6)
Berne (82)
Bierstedt (77)
Blumer (36)
Bortner (6) (70)
Braithwaite and Pettit (65)
Caldwell (106)
Capote (24)
Cloward and Ohlin (86)
Cohen (85)
Cooley (36)
Cox (153)
Cressey (6)
Cronin (95)
Cullen and Gilbert (4) (6) (9) (25)
    (26) (81)
Devlin (152)
Ellis (129) (153)
Empey and Erickson (89) (153)
Festinger (83)
Fisse and Braithwaite (66)

Flowers (44)
Fogel (4)
Fox (116)
Geiger (38)
Gibbons (70) (93)
Glaser (36)
Goffman (19) (23) (49) (50) (80)
    (131)
Greenberger (107)
Gubrium (24)
Haeckel (2)
Hagedorn (145)
Hollin (80)
Hollingshead (133)
Jacobs (142)
Karmen (111)
Kesey (19) (23)
Krisberg/Austin (5)
Lindzey (79) (80) (93)
Livingston (31)
Loomis and Loomis (36)
Lorenz (97)
MacIver (45)
Mackey, Miller, and Fredericks
    (49) (88) (129)
Matza (8) (11) (20) (22) (32) (110)
    (131) (153)
McClosky and Schaar (89)

Subject Index

actor-role congruency fallacy, 6,49,152
aggregative fallacy, 6,49
alchemy of police experience, 86
Alinsky, Saul, 121
anomy theory, 89
assertiveness training, 139
bad seed, 92
Baron von Munchausen effect, 157
behavioralism, 80
booty, 114
business model, 104
caveats of definition, 47
censorship, 63
centralization/decentralization of power, 154
Chaos theory, 96-98
Chicago School, 2-4
client centered therapy, 82
cognitive dissonance, 83
collective representations, 112
communicating skills, 35,37
concentration effects, 142
confidentiality, 61,64,65
containment theory, 66, 76
counter transference, 79
de-institutionalization, 24,25

delinquency definition, 44
delinquent subculture, 85,87,88
depoliticize, 154
detached workers, 85
deterrence, 66
dialectic, 83
dissonance, 83-84
doppelganger effect, 92
Dramatization of evil, 43
dual career, 28
due process, 117
eclecticism, 81
ecological fallacy, 6,49
Empire system, 23,24
equilibrium model, 83
eunomia, 89
family and delinquency, 94
female offenders, 70
Gallegos *vs* Colorado, 116
generalized other, 132, 136
Gibault School, 49
Goetz, Bernhard, 115
hidden delinquency, 46
Hurst, Wm Randolph, 110
ideology of child welfare, 36
ideology of rehabilitation, 5
impressionistic delinquency, 45

ABOUT THE AUTHORS

William J. Mackey:
Dr. William J. Mackey is currently Professor of Sociology at the University of Wisconsin-La Crosse, where he has previously been department chair, teaching courses in delinquency, urban sociology, and the sociology of deviance. He previously was a Professor at Chicago's Archdiocesan Seminary (Quigley) from 1961-68.

During the decade of the nineteen-fifties, Dr. Mackey had been actively engaged in correctional practice, serving as a Juvenile Probation Officer in Cook County (Chicago) and as a field Parole Agent with the Northern District of Illinois for the Department of Public Welfare. Additionally he was a resident Assistant Superintendent at the Juvenile Correctional Facility of Cook County (Chicago) for almost nine years.

Dr. Mackey earned his B.S. and M.A. degrees at the University of Illinois; he took his doctorate degree at Loyola University. He was a student of the late Professors Louis Wirth, Donald Taft and Florian Znaniecki all mentioned in this monograph.

Janet Fredericks:
Dr. Janet Fredericks served as principal of an inner-city parochial school and as an administrator in the American Institute of Banking. She is currently Professor and Associate Chair, Department of Educational Foundations, Northeastern Illinois University, where she teaches courses in Educational Administration.

Her elementary and high school education were completed in Catholic institutions in Ohio and Illinois. Dr. Fredericks obtained her B.S.,M.Ed. and Ph.D. degrees from Loyola University of Chicago. Her M.A.L.S.was received from Rosary College Graduate School of Library Science, and her Post-doctorate was completed at Harvard University Graduate School of Education in administration and policy studies.

Dr. Fredericks completed the volume *The Educational Views of Lyndon Baines Johnson*, and has co-authored *Hosting the Foreign Student*; and *In Search of Quality: The Development, Status and Forecasts of Standards in Post-Secondary Education*. Her more recent work is *From the Principals Desk* (1991). She has published in several journals including *Educational Theory, Scholastica Vita* and *Education*.

Marcel A. Fredericks:

Dr. Marcel Fredericks is a professor in the Department of Sociology-Anthropology, Loyola University of Chicago. Dr. Fredericks obtained his School Certificate with distinction from the University of Cambridge and matriculated from the University of London, England. He received his Ph,.D. degree in medical sociology from Loyola University of Chicago. He established the Office of Research in Medical Sociology and has since served as its director.

Dr. Fredericks has twice been awarded a United States Public Health Service Fellowship for research and teaching at the Harvard University Medical School, and was later appointed research associate in pediatrics there.

With Dr. Paul Mundy he has written on medical and dental sociology, including *The Sociology of Health Care*; *The Making of a Physician*; *Making It in Med School*; *Health Care and Its Providers* ;*Health Care in Guyana: The Sociology Health Care in a Developing Nation*; *Dental Care in Society*;*The Sociology of Dental Health,* and the monograph *First Steps in the Sociology of Health Care: A Catalyst for Social Change*. Other books include: *Citizen Jesuit*; *Hosting of the Foreign Student*; *First Steps in Sociology, In Search of Quality: The Development Status and Forecast of Standards in Postsecondary Accreditation*, (in press) and *Steps in Sociology: The Use and Misuse of Sociological Concepts*. He has published in numerous professional journals including: *Teaching Sociology, Educational Researcher, Journal of Medical Education,* and *Social Science and Medicine* and the *International Journal of Social and Social Psychology*.